Reinventing Live

The Always-On Future of Events

Denzil Rankine

Marco Giberti

ANTHEM PRESS

Anthem Press
An imprint of Wimbledon Publishing Company
www.anthempress.com

This edition first published in UK and USA 2021
by ANTHEM PRESS
75–76 Blackfriars Road, London SE1 8HA, UK
or PO Box 9779, London SW19 7ZG, UK
and
244 Madison Ave #116, New York, NY 10016, USA

British Library Cataloguing-in-Publication Data
A catalogue record for this book is available from the British Library.

Library of Congress Control Number: 2020951570

ISBN-13: 978-1-78527-692-7 (Hbk)
ISBN-10: 1-78527-692-1 (Hbk)

This title is also available as an e-book.

Contents

Exhibits

Chapter 1

Introductions by the Authors

Denzil Rankine and Marco Giberti

Denzil

Having already written five books, I was sure I had my fill. But then my friend Marco and I met in Colorado in March, the day before the Covid shutdown. In the short 24 hours before I dashed to the airport to catch the last flight out to the UK, we discussed just about every topic under the sun. And while we debated how the global pandemic might affect the world and change our lives, work, businesses, and reality, we were in absolute agreement about one thing. The impact on the events industry would be brutal, relentless, and transformative.

Of course, we already had ideas about how events needed to change. The pandemic merely became the catalyst, triggering the biggest turning point in the history of the global events industry and causing organizers and suppliers to be collectively concerned about their survival. All the major players are being forced to examine their business models and make radical, sweeping, and painful changes to adapt. Everyone is looking for a path forward.

We both knew we wanted to share our thinking on the changes needed and what the future of events might look like, so the idea of this book was born.

Florent Jarry, and other great colleagues of mine at AMR International, have been passionate about the transformation of the events industry for some years. To facilitate new thinking, we hosted the "Transform" series of events and roundtables. We also created the Exhibitions 2.0 concept, which addresses not only why things must change, but delivers a roadmap for transition. We strongly believe there is another way to engage and delight customers, strengthen events, and earn better returns.

This work has been both exciting and frustrating. We are excited by all the opportunity including the long list of tasks, processes, and workflows that can be executed more efficiently. But we have also been frustrated that the speed of change has been so slow. Without a "burning platform," no events-industry equivalent of Google killing business-to-business (B2B) media or Amazon annihilating retail, there has been little impetus for profound structural change.

Although there have been positive, incremental changes and new ways of working before now, this is the pivotal moment in which bold strategies can transform event organizers into community catalysts—the next phase in the evolution of events. The transformation will not be easy or straightforward. New skills will be required, and some old, comfortable habits will have to be broken. Nevertheless, I am convinced that for those who want to embrace the new reality we find ourselves in, the events industry holds enormous potential.

Events are integral to how all business is conducted. This book looks at how we can modify the event model to accommodate a world that is fast-tracking to the future and pave the way for a new vanguard of Millennial and Gen Z leaders who see the world through a much different lens than the generations before them.

It is fulfilling to help organizers, associations, service providers, venues, and investors navigate the terrain of this now fast-changing landscape. I, along with my colleagues at AMR, am excited to finally be at the forefront of the evolution of the industry we have inhabited for decades.

Marco

When I co-wrote *The Face of Digital* with Jay Weintraub in 2017, our primary goal was to organize our thoughts as entrepreneurs and investors in events and event technology. We also wanted to share our perspectives with industry leaders about different ways technology could help improve processes and solve problems.

Only three years later, when the urge to write another book came over me, the whole industry and world had changed in many ways. So, I decided to partner with my friend Denzil who has spent his career as a strategic consultant, building AMR as a globally trusted and respected consulting firm in the events industry. His experience is a perfect complement to my tenure as an entrepreneur and operator building start-ups from scratch to exit in the media, events, and tech industries and the decade of work in my investment and advisory firm, Vesuvio Ventures.

This book is predicated on the idea that events were built to succeed hundreds of years ago, but they are built to fail in the twenty-first century unless event organizers are ready to reinvent themselves. Comparing events of yesterday to those of today is like comparing print magazines to the iPad or a VHS tape to Netflix. The concept is valid, but the form factor is outdated.

Online purchasing is replacing brick-and-mortar retail and Amazon is eating the world. Similarly, many events will soon become casualties unless event owners rethink the value proposition of their events. The event industry needs to accelerate change if it wants to grow and keep a relevant share of the marketing budget of leading corporations.

The future of events is a fascinating topic for us. From sports, music festivals, and business-to-consumer (B2C) events to B2B trade shows and corporate meetings, the events industry is a massive channel that touches billions of people worldwide every week, online and face to face. And almost every single industry member and category is being disrupted.

I believe that events, in general, will not disappear. They will continue to be a powerful marketing and experience channel, as well as the first point of contact between many buyers and brands. But with new buyers and sellers becoming increasingly entrenched in digital technologies, the cravings for better and more productive live-event experiences will increase.

There are a wide variety of challenges facing events. Online product sourcing is becoming more accessible and more efficient thanks to new digital players and existing technologies. A new generation of marketers is leveraging technology for buyer–seller matchmaking and growing new customer communities outside the framework of in-person events.

But in the end, neither technology nor digital strategies are the most important changemakers. Boards and investors must push for the right leadership and accept a culture of experimentation, iteration, and change. Allowing failure, learning, and ultimate success means that effective leaders can challenge the *status quo*, regularly creating new concepts that add value for their vertical community stakeholders.

Finally, I decided to co-write this book because I have some things to say and many things to learn. After decades of work in different businesses and industries, I'm honestly convinced this is the time to "unlearn what we have learned" (as we say at the beginning of Chapter 7) and learn again with a fresh and humble attitude. Hopefully, sharing my own opinions and ideas will spark new conversations and help effect positive change.

I sincerely hope that readers will learn from our mistakes, bypass failure, and think differently about opportunities and challenges in their businesses and careers. If this is the case, the time and energy spent writing this book will have been a fantastic journey and an excellent way to assist the events industry with its evolution.

How to Use This Book

We have written this book as a guide for anyone interested in the future of events. You do not have to read every chapter, please feel free to dip in and out. At the end of each chapter we draw conclusions, hoping to provide you with some clear takeaways.

We are not trying to predict when the Covid crisis will end and we are not dealing in detail with the financial pain that is it causing. Instead we are looking ahead to how events will be changed in the future. We are highlighting changes in business models, and particularly which ones will emerge and flourish.

Most likely, events are experiencing more change now than they will at any other time in our lives. The industry continues to change as we write. So, we ask that you forgive us for anything that falls out of date rapidly. We will be publishing the second edition 12 months after the first, so we can revise our thinking as we progress through the crisis.

Please keep up to date with developments at www.reinventinglive. com. We will be providing updates on a regular basis and you can also provide feedback or share ideas.

Acknowledgements

Denzil

I am lucky to be inspired by my soulmate, Lucyann Barry. Although no longer in the events industry, her insights into what is broken and possible are extraordinary. Her help and support are invaluable.

We have also had tremendous support from friends, new and old across the events industry. We have asked you questions and tested ideas. Without your patience and your sharing we would not have been able to complete this work. Thank you, all.

Marco

To my wife Poly for her patience during long hours writing this book, and many years of intense career. But more important for being my partner in life and building our family, my most important achievement in life by far. To my dear children Luca, Micaela, and Francesca who are the ones who give me purpose and meaning to my life.

With so many changes (finally) happening, it was exciting to go back to a "research and academic mindset" to learn, investigate, and brainstorm with bright people about my business passions. I want to thank all of them for their feedback and ideas. Sincerely. We have many case studies and testimonials from industry leaders that shared their time, experiences, and lessons learned with us, and we hope that our readers will benefit from them. Your names are included in each quote or case study. Thank you!

Chapter 2

Summary

"What is now proved was once only imagined."
William Blake

It is now a mistake for an event organizer to think that it is primarily an event organizer.

This is not just because of Covid, although the pandemic has accelerated the wide range of changes already in motion. *The Face of Digital* referenced death by one thousand cuts and the urgent need for event organizers to engage digital technologies to improve their events and support their communities more effectively. This is now playing out, and more.

The digital revolution devastated business publishing. It also had some impact on events, although the effect was barely noticeable pre-Covid when the events market was reasonably robust and highly lucrative. Events earned good margins for stakeholders for many years. But the cat is now out of the bag as the primary group of paying customers—exhibitors—is not particularly satisfied.

Everyone now has an explosion of choice beyond the traditional town square market. New generations of business buyers want consumer-like experiences in everything they do. They expect instant search results on their devices and challenge how their time is spent. Corporate event marketers expect performance, measurability, and Return on investment (ROI) from their event investments as they assess the near-bewildering range of channels and choices available to reach their customers.

Railroads made the mistake of thinking they were in the railroad business. More important than running trains on time was creating value for customers by moving people and goods according to their needs and doing it effectively between destinations. In fact, they were in the transportation business. We think that event organizers should not see themselves as pure organizers. Their role is to facilitate—business, connections, education, and advocacy.

An event is a powerful tool in the arsenal of organizers. It is not their purpose. They can build trust face to face at an annual celebration of the industry, but they also need to keep those relationships alive all year long. Digital platforms offer the way to do that.

Pre-Covid, we started to see a bifurcation of the industry with the more sophisticated organizers beginning to use data and digital tools to enhance events. But the Covid-shock to the system demonstrates that they did not do enough. With the tide suddenly out, organizers appear to have been swimming naked. Communities still need business, connections, education, and advocacy, but event organizers are hardly able to help.

Of course, the Covid-shock is exceptional. We know that events recover from shocks, such as SARS, ash clouds, and other black swan events. But with the industry hitting a brick wall, customers being forced to make other choices and a set of new norms emerging, we are witnessing accelerated changes in customer expectations and behaviors. More importantly, the door has opened wider for alternatives to in-person events.

We have already seen outsiders such as Web Summit and Money 2020 create communities with new approaches. That's just the beginning. Now, we will see community building extend way beyond the event, as well as the emergence of more pure play digital businesses, which have earned the right to play in events.

The business and personal experience at events will also change massively. Community managers will become considerably more effective at facilitating the right connections and delivering opportunities. Event organizers will deploy a wide range of digital tools throughout the customer journey, before events, in and around events, and after them. Digital platforms that have developed highly engaged communities will add events as a seamless extension of their services. Winners will enable the success of their served markets.

Today's organizers need to adapt to being more than just organizers. Their challenge will be to translate trusted brands, market knowledge, attendee databases, industry-supplier databases, and content into meaningful platforms that emulate and improve what we do in the physical world online. This means hybrid online-offline-online platforms will prompt communities to interact in many new ways.

The event organizers that will be successful in the new world will be those that figure out what business they are in. Railroads or transportation, events or value-adding community catalysts? They will change mindsets throughout their organizations. For many, success up to now has rested on strong organizing skills and good marketing, with their blockbuster events protected by barriers to competition. They will have to become genuinely customer-first with new talent and a new culture.

There is no shortage of capital attracted to opportunities across the ecosystem, including events, event tech, and, of course, the digital platforms that may increasingly become disruptors. Many investors have made excellent returns already, encouraging plenty more waiting in the wings. The influx of financiers, with their combination of smarts and prospects for disruption, will accelerate change.

Event tech will be a critical ingredient in the new world. For example, business applications, such as matchmaking, have remained relatively nascent due to the complexity of needs across communities and event types compared to consumer applications such as ticketing. In a "chicken and egg" conundrum, pre-Covid organizers were slow to innovate or accelerate their use of event tech in the absence of a burning platform. We now have that burning platform, and an era of transformation has begun in which technology will play a starring role.

Success will lie with organizations that empower their served markets using a combination of activities and services, both digital and physical. They will deliver substantive outcomes in ways that are efficient, enjoyable, and enriching for all participants. A pure play event, even if it's a blockbuster, will appear monochrome against Technicolor experiences that offer a full range of surround-sound options.

Chapter 3

Events up to 2020

"Your margin is my opportunity."

Jeff Bezos

From about 500 BC, the Forum Magnum in Rome was used for the buying, selling, and trading of goods, and for business dealings, educational purposes, and social gatherings.

Much has changed in the last 2,500 years, but these human requirements have not. When we look at the sophisticated landscape of event types, facilities, and technologies that support or challenge in-person events today, we need to remember that they only exist because humans need to work, learn, and connect with others. Events have survived and thrived as they have consistently fulfilled fundamental and current market needs.

Event Formats

The focus of this book is B2B events and, to a lesser extent, consumer events. Exhibitions have been the stalwarts of the B2B sector (we draw on many examples from them in this book), but there is a multitude of other event formats that also exist. We describe the major event types in Exhibit 3.1.

We don't cover live entertainment, sports, or eSports in this particular tome, but we do reference fan events such as New York Comic Con as they have audiences as dedicated as any you will find at business events and lessons learned from them can cross over. We include consumer exhibitions as they have much in common with trade events, despite their typically lower profitability.

Exhibit 3.1 Events industry segmentation and definitions

Meetings and Incentives	Conventions	Exhibitions	Entertainment
Meetings The coming together of individuals to confer or carry out a particular activity	**Conference** Participatory meetings to facilitate information sharing	**Tradeshow (B2B)** Trade (including retail) / business focused events where companies promote products and services and build networks	**Live entertainment, concerts and festivals** Large-scale B2C events, typically featuring musical performances, performing art, attractions, etc
Incentives Meeting as part of a program offered to its participants to reward performance	**Congress** Large scale gathering connected to a defined group or association with peer review content	**Consumer exhibition (B2C)** Events for the public (direct to consumer) where products and services are displayed / sold	**Live sports** Sports held in indoor arenas in front of a live audience e.g. boxing, table tennis, basketball
	Confex Conference with an attached exhibition element		**eSports** B2C events where an audience watches highly-skilled video game players compete in tournaments
	High-touch events Leadership forums and 1-2-1 events		

☐ Our focus   ⬚ Peripheral

Source: AMR International

The main purpose of consumer events is to entertain the public and offer exhibitors an opportunity to sell products and build brand loyalty. Successful consumer event organizers trade on exceptional personal experiences and high levels of engagement among participants. B2B events have more complex value propositions than consumer events. Broadly, they aim to facilitate business, education, and connections. Experience (more an outcome of participation), although less important in B2B events, must be positive. B2B events also need to be easy to use and provide measurable results.

In the past, personal experience has taken a back seat in business events. But now participants are less tolerant of the gap between user experiences in their personal lives and those in their business lives.

The Events Ecosystem

While the ecosystem is complex, we see that organizers sit at the center. They can be independent or integrated with venues (Exhibit 3.2). Organizers can own the intellectual property (IP), i.e., the event brand, or they can be contracted to organize the event on behalf of the event owner or a brand. Organizers may produce events for a profit or, as in the case of corporate events, fulfill other purposes, such as promoting their brand.

- **Event organizers** typically hold the primary relationships. They contract with venue operators, service providers, and participants. Organizers, whether for-profit or not for-profit, need to be good at brand management, marketing, sales, and organizing.
- **Venue operators** provide space and selected services to make the event successful.
- **Service providers** offer myriad services to organizers, venues, and participants; they support the event operation and enhance the exhibitor and attendee experience. Very broadly, we can split services into two groups: manual services, such as freight handling or booth construction and digital services like registration or matchmaking.
- **Integrated providers** often cover the full spectrum of the events industry including event organization, venue operation and event-related services.

Exhibit 3.2 Events industry ecosystem

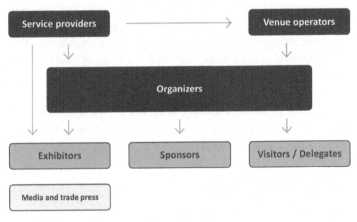

Source: AMR International

- **Delegates, attendees, exhibitors, and sponsors** are the participants. They use events to meet specific business goals, such as lead generation.
- **Media and trade press** support events and can play a central role in the ecosystem.

The Resilience of Exhibitions

Over the past two decades, exhibitions have led growth and performance across the events industry. AMR International's annual Globex Market Report and Forecast consistently described growth in the high single digits (except during the financial crisis of 2008) and recently estimated a pre-COVID growth rate of 5.5 percent per annum in a market sized at $39 billion globally. With growth exceeding Gross Domestic Product (GDP) and strong cash flow, world-leading private equity funds lined up to back the sector, kicking off an intense period of acquisitions.

During the same time, other segments of media and entertainment—exhibition industry cousins—began to evolve. The Digital Revolution pummeled traditional media, especially print. Many brands that had traditionally exhibited in and sponsored exhibitions chose to engage customers directly, fomenting the meteoric rise of direct-to-consumer (DTC) and fan events. In entertainment, rock bands, both new and aging, increasingly went on tour as their earnings from recordings were disrupted and eSports emerged as a new category.

Yet, in what appeared to some as a parallel universe, B2B and B2C exhibitions plodded along as analog wonders. Most organizers ignored both the warning signs and potential of digital, which accounted for only 2 percent of exhibition industry revenue, mostly in the form of sponsored email and online advertising. Technology had not yet evolved enough to replace the in-person experience; so, digital threats were limited to the replacement of some conferences with e-learning-type content. Digital tools were used mostly to plan, promote, and enhance events. But up to 2020, nearly 80 percent of revenues still came from selling booths (real estate on an exhibition floor).

Exhibit 3.3 Exhibition industry revenue split

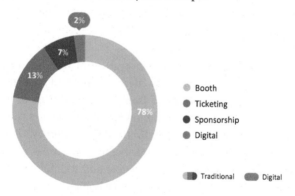

Underpinning this confidence in events was strong evidence that the industry delivered added value to its customers. Oxford Economics conducted a survey in 2017 that assessed the level of business sales generated by businesses events. It was calculated to be $2.5 trillion.

The survey went on to determine that the $1.5 trillion of total GDP supported by global business events would rank the sector as the 13th largest economy globally. This makes it larger than the economies of countries, such as Australia, Spain, Mexico, Indonesia, and Saudi Arabia.

Profitability

For the most part, events are highly lucrative. Strong margins are achievable as leading events can carve out exclusive positions with so-called must attend status, bringing together the movers and shakers of an industry in one place.

Also, customers are highly fragmented and very few are fully aware of the high margins achieved by event organizers. Most tolerate robust pricing, although some feel like hostages, compelled to participate despite limited return on investment.

Trade show organizing is the most lucrative part of the market. Exhibit 3.4 shows the weighted margins organizers achieve based on the latest data available before 2020.

In the 1990s, there was some convergence of the wide range of earnings before interest, taxes, depreciation and amortization (EBITDA) margins. New blood from other industries, as well as increased levels of private equity ownership, brought a theme of professionalization and industrialization to the industry, which led to margin improvement. Forward-looking organizers started to deploy improved management practices and technology enabled operating models. Some had unsustainably high margins, such as Emerald's 50 percent EBITDA, and were unable to maintain those profit levels after a period of underinvestment.

Many trade shows are owned by trade associations. In the United States, about two-thirds of the TSNN Top 250 list of largest exhibitions are association owned. Overall, associations operate on a not-for-profit basis in the interests of their members. But as the

Exhibit 3.4 Tradeshow organizer margins

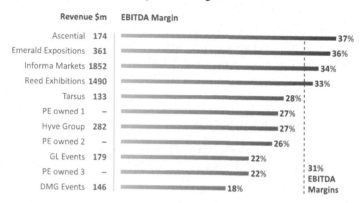

	Revenue $m	EBITDA Margin
Ascential	174	37%
Emerald Expositions	361	36%
Informa Markets	1852	34%
Reed Exhibitions	1490	33%
Tarsus	133	28%
PE owned 1	–	27%
Hyve Group	282	27%
PE owned 2	–	26%
GL Events	179	22%
PE owned 3	–	22%
DMG Events	146	18%

31% EBITDA Margins

Source: Latest available company reports, AMR analysis

events typically provide the lion's share of income for associations, they are highly motivated to make money from them to fund their other activities such as lobbying.

Margins in the conference sector vary but are typically below those of trade shows. Corporate meetings and customer events are not positioned as money makers; they are run to serve the business and foster relationships. Many have high production standards and are considered to be an investment in the brand or the attendees.

Most venues worldwide are funded by some version of local authorities. Their purpose is oriented primarily toward creating economic impact rather than delivering profit. This explains why, for example, tenancy costs in Germany are materially lower than in the UK. Those venues that are profit-oriented demonstrate that EBITDA margins of more than 20 percent are achievable.

Margins in service provision vary. They certainly can be attractive but are generally lower than those from event organizing or running profit-oriented venues.

As we all know, scaled technology businesses can enjoy very attractive margins. However, in the case of event tech, many applications require relatively high levels of customization and human capital inputs, which hold back their margins from the levels of pure software and SaaS businesses. We will look at this category in greater detail later.

Investment in the Sector

Investors fell in love with events. They liked the high margins, very strong cash flows, the limited need to invest, and relatively high recurring revenues.

By various measures, Blackstone is the world's largest private equity fund. It has invested in each of the major event industry segments (Exhibit 3.5).

Exhibit 3.5 Blackstone investments in events

Investment	Category		Position
Clarion	Organizer	Combined with Global Sources, another Blackstone investment	#4 globally
NEC	Venue	Major investment and transformation	#1 UK
PSAV	Services (AV)	Acquired Encore, another scaled player	#1 globally

Source: Blackstone, AMR analysis

Wilma Jordan, CEO and Founder of JEGI Clarity, a global investment bank told us "The decade 2010–2019 began with the ending of the Great Recession and ended with anticipation of ongoing growth and evolution of the Global Events Industry. During that period approximately $40.0 billion was invested by European and North American entities in Events-related businesses ranging from B2B to B2C Events, Facilities, Services and Technology."

JEGI data shows that

- Public Companies invested $19.7 million—Publicly Quoted Event Operators made a total investment of $15.8 billion on In Person events—including $12.1 billion on Trade Shows together with a further $3.7 billion on Confexes and Conferences. Other Public Companies invested $2.8 billion in Events Services and $1.1 billion in Consumer Events
- Private Equity Funds made a total investment of $18.0 billion. This included $7.8 billion on In Person events—$6.3 billion in Trade Shows and $1.5 billion in Confexes and Conferences. They also invested heavily in Events Services ($8.1 billion) and Consumer Events ($2.1 billion)
- Other investors—mainly private companies—invested $2.4 billion.

Wilma continued "Large amounts of available, cheap investment capital together with further equity investment helped fuel the consolidation of the Events industry. Detailed financial data on Private Equity Funds performance on their Events industry investments is not available publicly. Nonetheless, the on-going enthusiasm being shown by PE for new platforms and add-on acquisitions across the Event industry suggests that the medium term returns on a three to four year investment hold period have been achieving the PE Funds' target of 3 x invested capital."

There are many dozens of examples of value creation across all ownership categories in the events industry—publicly listed, private equity and private shareholders. We will look at Clarion Events as it is a good example, as well as an interesting story.

CASE STUDY
CLARION EVENTS – VALUE CREATION

Summary

Clarion has had five private equity owners over 20 years, each supporting growth as the business has risen from a local UK organizer to the fourth largest globally.

Early Days

The business has a long history. It started in 1948 and achieved little growth over 50 years under different owners, including a shipping group. In 1999 P&O Events was the unprofitable organizing arm of London's Earls Court venue; management had the opportunity to buy the business, backed by private equity.

Private Equity Ownership

Each of Clarion's five private equity owners since 1999 has added value to the business. In that period, Clarion has grown from 30 employees to over 2,000 worldwide, from 14 events to over 200 events plus digital media.

The group has moved its focus from consumer events to B2B events. It has also significantly expanded its geographic reach from regional to national in the UK, then to international and finally to global.

The table below summarizes the story.

Owner	Entry	Revenue £m	Profit £m	Strategy
Candover	1999	n/a	n/a	• Separation from venue
Hg Capital	2004	35	3.5	• Operate beyond London, through JVs with UK regional venues, SECC and NEC • Major acquisition of ICE, the International Casino exhibition • Strong organic growth
Veronis Suhler Stevenson	2008	60	10	• Internationalization via acquisition of Confex producers plus International events, e.g., DSEI • Continued organic growth

Owner	Entry	Revenue £m	Profit £m	Strategy
Providence	2014	180	20	• Create strong footprint in the US through acquisition of Urban Expo • Buy and build in existing portfolios
Blackstone	2017	250	50	• Large US and Asia acquisitions, Pennwell and Global Sources • Continuation of buy and build • Organic growth

Simon Kimble, Executive Chairman explains "Each private equity owner brought different skills and support that was appropriate to our needs at the time, above all a federal, developmental style has enabled us to flourish."

Professionalization

Pre-Covid events continued to deliver strong profits with growth partly fuelled by acquisition. However, in recent years takeover opportunities started to dwindle, and those available were more contested and more expensive. With slower growth rates, players found that they had to work just a bit harder to deliver results to their masters.

Tim Cobbold, an engineer and CEO of UBM before its sale to Informa in 2017, famously used the term "industrialization" to describe his changes. He moved from an operating model that was highly federated in the direction of much more centralized control.

Leaders such as Reed Exhibitions also made major investments in systems, seeking to benefit from economies of scale and using selected common practices to create efficiencies. Data analytics took a place on the agenda. Sophisticated pricing practices came in, giving some an immediate uplift in performance. However, compared to other industries that came under severe pressure such as retail, the adoption of analytics and sophisticated pricing has been very slow to evolve in exhibitions.

Private equity investors with their cross-industry experience, rosters of experts, and their improvement formulas used their board seats to make relatively far-reaching changes, pushing for new ways of working more aggressively than many other owners.

We started to see divergence in the industry in the mid-2010s. While a set of players took more sophisticated approaches and benefitted from scale. Others made fewer changes, either held back by ownership structures that did not prioritize investment, or because they did not recognize the challenges facing the sector. Most in this second category sailed on buoyed by the still unreplaced need for face-to-face industry gatherings. A notable number failed. CeBIT and Interbike were clear leaders in their markets before collapsing.

In March 2020, we saw the world enter suspended animation. Nonetheless, investors continued to support the sector financially with debt while equity holders in private equity backed businesses held their positions. Investors continue to believe in the fundamental advantages events provide in helping communities to meet their needs—business, education, and connection.

Analog World

Before 2020, events largely operated in an analog world. The Internet brought efficiency, but limited disruption. The cost of attendee promotion decreased as brochures were eliminated and show catalogs went online. Audio-visual activations became more sophisticated and some notable event-tech start-ups gained traction. But there was no revolution. As other marketing channels were transformed through constant innovation and change, the face-to-face industry found that it hardly needed to evolve to continue to make an attractive living for all involved.

Thus, without a compelling need to innovate, event organizer research and development (R&D) budgets were at best limited. Event agencies and the major service providers pushed for improved participant experiences. Feeling less constrained by having to earn a profit, direct-to-customer events such as Salesforce's Dreamforce delivered most of the innovation. There was some experimentation and development money; however, much of it was focused on event launches. Some of the most noteworthy successes such as Web Summit, "Davos for geeks," and Money20/20 came from event-industry outsiders who prioritized translating participant needs into an event experience. In parallel, we saw the evolution of formats, richer content, more focused one-to-one networking and exclusive, "high touch" leadership events.

There were many brave attempts to bring events more comprehensively into the Digital Age. Notably UBM made several bold attempts at digital innovation, first with virtual events in 2007 and then later, under different leadership, with marketplaces. We are going to look at these stories as they illustrate the uphill battle of tech innovation pre-2020.

CASE STUDY
UBM'S VIRTUAL EVENTS DISAPPOINTMENT

Summary

UBM attempted to run virtual shows in the late 2000s. The initiative failed to gain traction as the events did not give customers what they wanted.

Context

In 2007, UBM acquired How Machines Work (HMW), a firm specializing in 3D interactive models, and combined it with UBM Studio, UBM's virtual-media team. UBM then launched a series of virtual events mostly focused in its content-heavy sectors such as IT and pharmaceutical.

UBM attempted to recreate the physical show visit experience virtually. There were virtual booths and products on display, background noise, and a bar area with bar noise to encourage networking.

The Outcome

UBM achieved some success, notably with the legacy Comdex brand that came with an acquisition. However, the overall initiative failed to gain traction and was wound down after several editions.

Lessons Learned

Meet the needs of customers

The computer game-like offerings did not work for the audience; they failed to facilitate the connection between buyers and sellers smoothly. The experience of virtual participation was vastly inferior to on-site participation.

> "We made the mistake to recreate the event virtually. The experience of walking around the virtual booths is nowhere near the real experience. You are trying to re-create the experience which is impossible to achieve." — ex-UBM executive

Instead of focusing on creating a digital replication of a tradeshow, UBM should have found tools that served the needs of customers. For transactional shows, these could be search platforms and e-directories for product discovery and other services such as matchmaking and content-sharing through webinars or white papers.

> "We needed to find the best way to match the value proposition that an event gives, that is the ability to connect and find buyers and suppliers. Online search and directories are the best way to do that."—ex-UBM executive

Solutions need to be adapted by event type. Content-heavy events call for a different set of tools compared to transaction-focused events.

> "What UBM could have done is create its own platform with 1:1 matchmaking, live conference and the connection of buyers of sellers in an Amazon like model—instead, we relied on the "digital venues" just like we relied on the live venues for hosting."—ex-UBM executive

Choose the Right Business Model

UBM tried various pricing strategies and found there was little useful "read across" from physical to virtual events. UBM was hampered by its success in selling space and sponsorship at shows and failed to establish a tailored and coherent pricing strategy for virtual events.

Some bundling with the associated physical show worked, although this also risked backfiring and taxing the main event.

In hindsight, UBM recognized that for a brand new, online-centric offering, a subscription-based model could help to drive exhibitor and attendee engagement all year round.

"If you start a virtual event from fresh, then the subscription model is the right way for both exhibitors and visitors to drive engagement all year round." – ex-UBM executive

Conclusions

UBM was too early. More recently, there have been massive advances in 3D technologies and were their attempts executed in 2020 the generational change could potentially have boosted adoption and participation.

UBM failed as it had to rely on avatar technology and struggled to step outside its trade show mindset. It should have put the business needs of customers first, and the experience second.

UBM was prepared to experiment and invest in R&D.

"Surely every large events operator needs to do R&D—maybe UBM would have done better to keep persisting, keep failing . . . keep trying . . ."—ex UBM CEO

Despite the disappointing outcome, UBM learned important lessons and continued to shape its online proposition. The teams involved in these initiatives are creating successful virtual events under other roofs in the 2020s.

The Effect on Event Technology

A decade on and under different leadership, UBM attempted a major innovation with its O2O2O marketplace initiative, partnering with Alibaba. This also ended in disappointment; once again the firm was ahead of its time. We look at that case study in Chapter 7.

The UBM failure and others reinforced the thinking of many industry insiders that "events are different." It became common to cite the failure of virtual events as a reason not to experiment or adopt new technology.

A culture of innovation, in particular with new forms of event tech, existed only in pockets. Regardless, hundreds of event tech suppliers continued to eke out an existence, waiting for their moment when the industry would embrace their offerings wholeheartedly.

There was, however, major investment in other technology, in systems such as customer relationship management (CRM), marketing automation, and database platforms. These systems improved the "back end". They were also important in consolidating operations across internal groups that had created fiefdoms or grown by acquisition. There was nothing exceptional about this investment, however. The same or more was happening in most other industries, regardless of their offerings, geography, or ownership structure.

So, that sets the scene. We will now go on to look in greater depth at why events needed to change before the Covid crisis hit.

Conclusions

- The events sector is diverse and fragmented; it was robust pre-Covid
- The sector has traditionally been highly attractive to investors
- Events have been through a period of sustained growth, consolidation, and professionalization
- The digital revolution had a limited impact on events, almost as if operating in a parallel universe
- There was limited investment in event technology

Chapter 4

Why Events are Changing

"There will be a reckoning of the real value of events."
Paul Miller, CEO Questex

It is easy to say the reason events are changing is, of course, Covid. But we think there were already headwinds before the pandemic.

Covid stopped the events industry in its tracks in 2020. As it re-emerges from the Covid reset, the industry will reflect the pressures it was under in the preceding decade, as well as the new ways of working the crisis brought about.

Will Events Be Disintermediated?

First, let's address the question of whether events are here to stay or not. People immersed in and dependent on events universally believe that in-person events are irreplaceable. So, we need to check some proof points to be sure that we are not asking chickens whether they plan to vote for Colonel Sanders.

The first proof point comes from the technology sector. AMR International estimates that customer events run by tech firms were growing at 8–10 percent per annum pre-Covid, that's almost twice the growth rate of the rest of the industry. If tech firms were planning to be the disruptors, it was not evident. In fact, some of their success was decelerating the growth of third-party events, such as tradeshows and conferences.

We spoke with the CMO of one of the tech giants that could be seen as a potential disintermediator. We heard of strong support for events and no plans for disruption. "Events create visceral connection and energy in a group of people that becomes infectious because of the centre that they create."

The next place to look is at the customers of in-person events in the light of the thousands of events canceled due to the pandemic. Event organizers that depend on events for revenues and profits needed to retain liquidity, so they retained the exhibitor fees, marshaling various arguments and incentives to do so. Only a small proportion of their customers required their money back. Most were prepared to roll the dice, shifting their investments to the next edition, whenever that may be. This represents a continuing strong vote of confidence for events.

There are numerous surveys showing that events are ranked as the most effective channel by B2B marketers, often topping the poll at 70 percent when given multiple choices. Exhibit 4.1 shows one example.

Exhibit 4.1 B2B demand generation tactics

Percentage of survey respondents that selected each demand generation tactic as successful

"Which engagement tactics were most successful for you in 2018 in terms of generating qualified leads for the top of the funnel?"

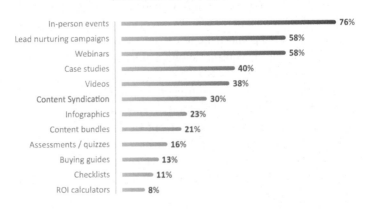

Tactic	%
In-person events	76%
Lead nurturing campaigns	58%
Webinars	58%
Case studies	40%
Videos	38%
Content Syndication	30%
Infographics	23%
Content bundles	21%
Assessments / quizzes	16%
Buying guides	13%
Checklists	11%
ROI calculators	8%

Source: Demand Gen Report

Note: Based on a survey of more than 150 B2B marketing practitioners (most US based), c. 50% from companies with over $50m revenue

If we look at investors, we see (at the time of writing this book) their enduring confidence in the sector. True, the share prices of quoted groups focused entirely on events collapsed, but the private equity owners of events groups held firm, making follow-on investments. Furthermore, the separate category of debt providers that lent alongside private equity did not jump ship. Many had the opportunity to do so on secondary markets, but they remained confident that the events industry would come back.

On the attendee side, data from research firm Explori, the Global Association of the Exhibition Industry (UFI), and the Society of Independent Show Organizers (SISO) found a high level of loyalty, albeit among users of events:

> "Of those who come to business events as delegates, *90% felt they had been negatively impacted* as a result of not being able to attend events. Nine out of ten felt that alternative solutions such as *virtual events were not as effective* in meeting their professional needs as live events." Explori UFI and SISO research 2020[1]

So, we can expect business events to continue. But in such a diverse industry, we will see a lot of changes across sectors, event types, and event objectives.

To understand what the industry will look like in the near future, we have to look at the pressures it was under before the pandemic. We need to do that because when the reset comes it can surface all sorts of grievances. It is best for them to be aired and then fixed.

---

[1] https://www.explori.com/en-gb/global-visitor-insights-2019   https://www.ufi.org/wp-content/uploads/2019/01/UFI_Explori_Global_Visitor_report_2018-1.pdf

Generational Change

Generational change is impacting events. Digital-native buyers and sellers are less tolerant of clunky experiences. They expect to be connected, engaged and to instantly find the information they need precisely when it is relevant. Millennials who grew up with home internet access, smartphones, social media, and online shopping have brought their online buying habits and expertise into B2B buying. They are not necessarily following the paths of their older peers.

Millennials, in particular, will play a large role in the transition of the events industry. Pew Research reported that as of 2017, Millennials represent the largest category of the workforce, overtaking Baby Boomers and Gen Xers. From 2020–2025 they will represent 40 percent of the North American workforce (43 percent globally) with Gen X in a declining second position, according to NGA, a global HR group. Various studies including one from Merit, a brand agency, report over 75 percent of Millennials working in B2B have involvement in buying.[2] Millennials bring their digital education as the Google generation to the leadership roles they are assuming. This will require a more sophisticated value proposition and ROI tools from event owners.

Gen Z is the touchscreen generation. They were born touching screens for reading newspapers, magazines, blogs, and books; watching movies and TV; playing games, listening to music, and so many other things. Touchscreens are their way of life. They are now participating in events, some aghast at the old-world experience (Exhibit 4.2).

---

[2] https://www.pewresearch.org/fact-tank/2018/04/11/millennials-largest-generation-us-labor-force/   https://madewithmerit.com/millennials-make-73-per-cent-purchasing-decisions-b2b/

Exhibit 4.2 Generation definitions

Generation	Born	Age in 2025
Generation Z	1997 and onwards	≤28
Millennials	1981–1996	29–44
Generation X	1965–1980	45–60
Baby Boomers	1946–1964	61–79
Silent Generation	1928–1945	80–97

Mass Digitization

The modern world is now digital. Smart phone penetration is complete. As a result, video and social media have become preferred tools. Amazon has driven up everyone's expectations for seamless customer experiences in both B2C and B2B e-commerce.

The ways buyers use technology to research products and services, qualify vendors, and make purchases has changed the game for marketers and product managers. Most buyers now use digital channels in the initial phase of any new procurement. Those trying to reach them will employ tactics including search engine optimization (SEO), social media, and content strategy.

Today, the buying process involves more self-service and discovery than ever before. According to Forrester, 68 percent of B2B customers prefer to self-serve and complete independent research online (Exhibit 4.3). Research by McKinsey shows a rapid shift to self-serve from directed channels across the purchasing process.[3]

---

[3] https://go.forrester.com/blogs/welcome-to-the-b2b-marketing-renaissance/

Exhibit 4.3 B2B buyers growing preference for self-serve

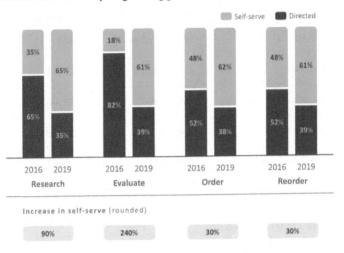

Buyers in general are omnichannel creatures. Their journey floats in and out of traditional and digital sales channels and the B2B buying process is anything but linear as customers move between self-serve and physical interactions as needed. We can be sure that when attendees arrive at an event, they are now far more informed and will be unimpressed with a nonresponsive, disconnected experience.

Questionable Value

Pre-Covid, customer satisfaction across business events was lacking particularly for marketers, the exhibitors, and sponsors.

One of the first actions of a CEO who came into the events industry was to conduct a touchpoint analysis of his paying customers. He was shocked to discover customers bombarded with sales calls, payment requests, and operational instructions. The customer experience is not always that bad; however, the cycle illustrated is not unusual (Exhibit 4.4).

Exhibit 4.4 Exhibitor sentiment through the event cycle

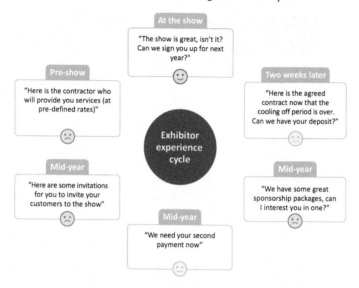

Another events group CEO summarized how he sees the industry:

> "Shareholders come first, then it's employees—and third in line are customers." CEO private equity backed event organizer

It is very normal for exhibitors to complain about the cost of participating in events and yet turn up again the following year. Globally, exhibitor retention rates are about 65 percent by volume and closer to 80 percent by value. The larger accounts are more loyal, in part because they are a partially captive customer set.

Explori, in association with UFI has measured the net promoter scores (NPS, the percentage of promoters minus the percentage of detractors) of exhibitors, the paying customers, across thousands of events. Their data supports exhibitor dissatisfaction (Exhibit 4.5).

As you can see, the Exhibitor NPS was negative: -17. Only one quarter of events in the sample had a positive NPS for exhibitors.

Exhibit 4.5 UFI Explori NPS survey

"Exhibitor advocacy is low across the globe: only 25% of shows have a positive Net Promoter Score (NPS). Globally, exhibitors rate the exhibitions they attend with a negative average NPS of -17." Explori Global Exhibitor Insights 2017

Attendees were more positive, with a score of +5. However, in the 2019 survey 25 percent of North American attendees reported trade shows to be getting worse.

"Whilst trade shows are the channel of choice for most business needs, visitors indicate their use of other channels will grow at a greater rate than their use of trade shows. 40% of respondents said their use of social media and online training would increase, vs. 28% who thought their use of trade shows as a channel would increase." Explori Global Exhibitor Insights 2019

ROI

Alternative channels, such as Google AdWords, for example, offer more measurable ROI. CMOs work in the world of measurability and the language of marketing qualified leads (MQL), sales qualified leads (SQL), cost per lead, and cost per opportunity. They quantify levels of engagement and hyper-target specific accounts, job titles, and geographies. CMOs assess marketing investments based on these types of metrics, calculating ROI across most of their channels. Events have been the exception.

Overall, events have largely been sold based on access to a promised audience. This is the same CPM (cost per thousand) basis that print publishers used as their common currency before their demise at the hands of Google.

As data and technology have evolved, it became possible to find ways to measure ROI for exhibitors and sponsors. However, a cocktail of restraints stood in the way, including infrastructures such as beacons, technical challenges and, most of all, the fear of sharing the feedback with customers. We have seen that organizer efforts to offer ROI measurement have mostly been in the tech sector as a reaction to customer demand, not as a progressive innovation.

In the retail sector, it is common to measure footfall, traffic patterns, and revenue per shelf foot and adjust offers and promotions to optimize performance. Tracking technologies are commonly deployed, and analytics are universal. At least some of these capabilities and expectations are spreading to events.

Hostages

In their research, Explori also found that a sizable proportion of exhibitors are hostages, exhibitors that feel they must exhibit even though they do not get tangible value. At least some of these are key accounts. It's a concern should they find alternatives (Exhibit 4.6).

Exhibit 4.6 Satisfaction—loyalty matrix

Source: UFI/Explori NPS research on 1000+ tradeshows

Return on time

Attendees are of course the even more important customer group. The good news is that the Explori research found them to have a positive NPS. Attendees have begun to scrutinize the value of events more closely. They are under increasing time and productivity pressure. Just as importantly, attendees are being offered alternate ways to achieve their objectives besides attending events.

Overall attendee numbers are not growing as fast as the industry and combined with data on time spent at events, analysis by AMR International shows that "total attendee time" is in very gradual decline. Thus marketers are neither getting the audience they require nor the time spent with target customers and prospects. If the organizer policy is to deliver fewer, better qualified attendees, they need to communicate that.

Corporate meeting attendees are just as short on time. In the Convene Meetings Market Survey, 31 percent of corporate meeting planners say they would reduce the number of hotel room nights if budgets had to be cut. In other words, their customers would appreciate the time savings of an abbreviated event.

Marketing Convergence and Alternatives

Events have long been a separate line item within marketing budgets and sometimes sales budgets. We are now moving to more joined-up approaches with the emergence of multichannel and omnichannel marketing. With CRM systems and marketing automation at the heart of sales and marketing efforts, marketing budget holders seek common standards.

Event participants were already being offered an increasing range of alternatives in the 2010s, mostly due to the continuing digital revolution. While events offer uniqueness of experience and some irreplaceable benefits, such as proximity and immersion, marketers and attendees were already on the hunt.

We all know that B2B print advertising has pretty much died. If we look at the reasons, as highlighted in AMR International's research for SISO in 2017, the list of advertiser grievances is similar to the complaints of event exhibitors—the lack of ROI, specific targeting, flexibility, and customer data (Exhibit 4.7).

Exhibit 4.7 Marketer expectations of print

Wants	Print	Sentiment
ROI	(x)	"Digital marketing enables brands to drive tangible ROI in real time. It's difficult to prove ROI with print." *– CEO, Large fashion brand*
Targeting	(x)	"We use digital advertising and set demographic parameters based off customer data. We can't be this targeted with print." *– Head of marketing, Small publisher*
Flexibility	(x)	"The performance of digital can be assessed in real time and feedback used to adjust strategies immediately rather than waiting for the next print run." *– Director of Global stores strategy, Large fashion brand*
Customer data	(x)	"Print cannot tell us anything about who our customers are." *– Marketing Manager, Large gift brand*

Direct to Consumer (DTC) CMOs told AMR that events are valued for some of their unique attributes, but that they are next in the firing line as they develop their channel strategies.

Sustainability

Sustainability has come onto the world agenda. Eighty percent of Millennials state that a company's environmental, social, and philanthropic efforts impact their purchasing decisions.[4]

The bad news is that business events have a poor track record, producing waste and requiring travel.

---

[4] https://askwonder.com/research/genz-and-millennials-corporate-social-responsibility-t7uqq3oot

Exhibit 4.8 Breakdown of a trade show in China

Source: Edwin van der Vennet, beMatrix

Fortunately, it is not the norm to use three mechanical diggers for the breakdown of an exhibition. Nonetheless, Exhibit 4.8 from a Chinese venue is frightening. Even without diggers, the level of waste events create is substantial. Although there is growth in modular systems, most booths are non-recyclable. All of the other disposable material, from carpets and signage to food service items and give-aways, contribute to environmental degradation as well.

Physical events are making moves to improve their green credentials. Easyfairs has been offering the all-in formula with reusable stands for well over a decade. Modular exhibit providers, such as beMatrix, continue to innovate their stands and venues like Viparis have embarked on serious environmental initiatives. But there is still a long way to go. The events industry is fortunate not yet to have caught the eye of serious environmental activists.

Travel is an increasingly sensitive environmental issue. Global annual air passenger traffic had been growing steadily at 5 percent per annum up to 2020. But then Swedish air travel started to decline pre-Covid as young environmental activist Greta Thunberg put *Flygskam* or "flight shaming" onto the agenda. Airline CEOs feared this would spread.

Now, forced choices have shown many people that perhaps all their travel was not necessary.

However, events do enjoy travel efficiency. The high number of meetings held at an event per air mile flown is a powerful argument to the participation of events in the fight against climate change.

Purely digital channels avoid all the problems of waste and travel. Proponents of hybrid and digital channels trumpet their environmental credentials in all the technology pitch decks we see, arguing to potential investors that their substantially better green credentials are a significant and important differentiator to face-to-face events.

When events return, organizers and venues will have the opportunity for an environmental reset. The list of opportunities is long, including more touchless, change in materials, less plastic, and so on.

Forced Choices

In February 2014, a London Underground strike closed part of the system. Due to the strike, many commuters were forced to experiment with different routes to their chosen regular routine. This forced choice led to a sizeable fraction of commuters finding better routes. Around 5 percent stuck with these new routes after the strike was over.[5]

Similarly, the Covid crisis forced event participants to make choices. Some will discover that the previously unconsidered alternative is much better than they had imagined.

It is too early to tell how business event budgets will be reset post-pandemic. Research by IEEE Globalspec in 2020 showed that about half of unused event budgets would remain unspent. Of the part

---

[5] http://cep.lse.ac.uk/pubs/download/cp455.pdf

reallocated, most would go to digital marketing, followed by content. We have already discussed research showing hotel nights to be a cost cutting target in business meetings, implying favorable conditions for scaled back or hybrid events.

Those countries that exited the lockdown first found that as 2020 progressed online retail was slipping back toward January penetration. As a very rough rule of thumb about half of the gains were already lost. At the time of writing it is too early to judge how much marketing spend will be reallocated away from events permanently, but it is reasonable to think that it will between this 50 percent and the 5 percent of London commuters who changed their preferences after the underground strike that led to forced choices.

Reduced Barriers to Entry

Suddenly the barriers to entry for new events have been lowered. In 2020, virtual events became an accepted norm for canceled in-person events, helping organizers to fill a gap and stay in touch with their communities. They also became a launch tool either for existing technology players or for challengers. The REMOTE event launched by a challenger in a previously impossible lead time has certainly earned the right to run again and to expand.

CASE STUDY
REMOTE, THE CONNECTED FACULTY SUMMIT

Pureplay virtual launch benefitting from reduced barriers to entry

Summary

Arizona State University (ASU) launched a highly successful virtual event in eight weeks with limited resources. ASU had neither a marketing budget nor a history of event organizing.

The Event

REMOTE: the connected faculty summit, a virtual event was launched to help higher education faculty and administrators design and deliver engaging online teaching material.

The event was created in eight weeks. It had seven streams, including numerous open Q&A sessions, workshops, and content presentations capped at 20 minutes. Further engagement and networking were facilitated by 34 topic-based chat rooms.

No Event Experience, No Marketing Budget

In addition to limited preparation time, ASU has deep sector knowledge in education but had no experience of organizing large-scale events. So, it leveraged the experience of events and education veteran and entrepreneur in residence former UBM CEO David Levin, several ASU foundation members, and a delivery partner, Questex. ASU had no budget allocated for marketing; this was done entirely through the sponsors.

The Outcome

With over 27,000 attendees, 34 percent of which spent over six hours online, the event was a success.

> "It was simply amazing what your team was able to pull off in such a short time. We were honoured to be a part of it." Elizabeth Stovall, Microsoft

Here are some more data points:

- Each presentation averaged over 2,000 viewers, with some seeing almost 10,000
- Each viewer participated in eight presentations on average
- Networking lounges saw over 22,000 viewers and attracted almost 5,000 posts
- Interactive Q&A sessions had up to 7,300 viewers at a time

The event established its position and will run again. It plans new adaptations across educational levels and also geographies.

Conclusions

- Virtual can be a game-changer with substantially reduced barriers and high levels of effectiveness:

    - Rapid speed to market
    - Very little financing
    - Extended audience reach
    - High levels of interaction

- Partnerships can be very powerful, combining excellence in brand, keynotes, content, database, and execution

In summary, we know that the global events industry was posting growth that was either in line with or above GDP and investors saw it as highly attractive. But events were already swimming against the current. Their unique qualities, including the proximity and immersion that they gave their customers, also allowed them to flourish despite their shortcomings.

Mike Rusbridge who led Reed Exhibitions for two decades summarized the situation as he and his long-time colleague Nick Forster see it:

"Coronavirus preys on people with existing conditions; how many events have existing conditions before the pandemic? The failure rate may be similar!" Mike Rusbridge, Former Executive Chairman, Reed Exhibitions

We argue that if your computer is crashed by a virus and needs a software update, when you restart it again, surely it's best to have an upgrade that deals with all of the former niggles and reflects your future needs. We think that the events industry should get that upgrade.

Conclusions

- Events had headwinds pre-Covid due to the expanding range of participant alternatives and the lack of value measurement
- Generational change is having a significant impact on buyer and seller behaviors
- Forced choices are accelerating changes
- Virtual events reduce the barriers to entry for would-be organizers
- Climate change and sustainability are largely unsolved problems in events
- The events industry needs to reset for the future, not the past

Chapter 5

Alternative Future Models for Events

Virtual, Hybrid, Platforms, and F2F

> *The old saying goes: "Pioneers take the arrows; settlers take the land."*

It's nice being a pioneer, but most of the time, it's also painful. The arrows mentioned in the old saying usually hurt and sometimes can kill you. There is absolutely nothing wrong with being a pioneer, but you can also learn from them, be a successful settler, and take the land.

Event Tech Is No Longer "Nice to Have"

There are many future models that organizers should research, understand, and analyze before resetting their events for the future. As with software companies, they can develop a MVP (minimum viable product) for specific new event formats, including virtual, hybrid, or face to face (F2F). Then they can test their customers' reactions, adjust, learn, rethink the model, and do it again until the right formula for a new event emerges. And, like it or not, they will have to keep repeating this process if they want the business to have a long and successful life.

Software companies can check and adjust their MVP daily if necessary. F2F event organizers accustomed to long event cycles (annual or even longer sometimes) need to think of different ways to activate MVP testing. Digital event extensions are still mostly linked to the annual cycle, and they can be easier to test than F2F events as they can be switched off and on more easily and carry less risk when they don't work well.

The value proposition of F2F events continues to be compelling and valuable and it remains a very productive marketing and business development investment for brands. Replacing F2F with technology is not easy. It is almost impossible if networking and commerce are essential event components. But complementing and improving in-real-life (IRL) experiences through digital technologies is possible and an excellent opportunity for organizers to add new revenue sources and added value to their events. In fact, digital is no longer a luxury for event organizers, and it's becoming a critical tool for survival. There are many opportunities for live and virtual-event experiences to join forces. As Waco Hoover, Founder of XLIVE, a leading event for the festival, sports, and music industry (now part of LDI, which Questex acquired), and an active investor and advisor in the events industry explained, "The B2C, festivals and sports event market was hit very hard by Covid. Fundamental changes and rethinking the business is a key priority. We are all forced to do things differently and experiment with new ideas. For example, there are three billion gamers worldwide, representing a massive opportunity for live entertainment to create new partnerships in sports and music. NASCAR created new engagement opportunities around eSports that have drawn audiences of 1M+ interacting with drivers as they compete in real time."

Event technology has been available for a couple of decades in some categories. Registration, data capture, and virtual events are a few examples. Yet, we have only experienced deep engagement and acceleration over the last five years. We can expect to see even more robust engagement and faster acceleration during the next decade.

We will go into more depth on the most important tech areas, categories, and key tech players generating innovation in the events space later in Chapter 6. But first, let's analyze alternative events models and the ways these models can use technology to generate

Exhibit 5.1 Event formats by era

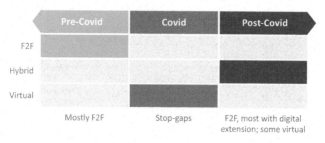

	Pre-Covid	Covid	Post-Covid
F2F			
Hybrid			
Virtual			
	Mostly F2F	Stop-gaps	F2F, most with digital extension; some virtual

innovation and better experiences. We will focus on F2F, virtual, and hybrid categories first. We will also share our thoughts on digital platforms and B2B marketplaces, as well as different ways for these events categories and activations to coexist, creating more and better opportunities for all event-industry stakeholders. Below, we show three eras and identify an event format that can take the lead in each one (Exhibits 5.1 and 5.2).

If you are an event organizer contemplating future models and, particularly, if you are thinking about combining formats into a hybrid approach, you need to find the formula that works best for your community. This type of innovation requires an entrepreneurial and flexible approach, experimentation and trial and error to validate the right format.

As Bob Priest Heck, CEO at Freeman told us, "Successful event organizers will be those who realize that they're not selling real estate but bartering with the currency of time. It's not about talking at a captive audience, but husbanding time spent with an audience in a way that engages and captivates. That's where the value is. This should be a relevant, cadenced dialog that extends year-round."

Face to Face

Hundreds of years in the making, the face to face value proposition continues to be robust and unique. We believe that trust is built

Exhibit 5.2 Event format definitions

Format	Delivery		Example duration (days)	Interactive streaming	Comment
	Physical	Digital			
F2F	Yes	No	2-5	No	In-person only
Virtual	No	Yes	1-3	Yes	Standalone, or can be part of hybrid
Hybrid	Yes	Yes	<365	Yes	In-person, plus digital extension(s) during the event or directly related to it during the year Extensions can be via: • Live streaming • **Digital platforms** • Virtual events

Digital tools (e.g. matchmaking): F2F = Yes, Virtual = Yes, Hybrid = Yes.

Digital platform (e.g. Data, Leadgen, B2B marketplace): F2F = No, Virtual = Unlikely, Hybrid = Preferably.

Note: Definition of an event: Two way interaction between people who can see each other live, either in person or via video.

in person, and the right meeting, experience, and context can help accelerate business opportunities. Despite the pros and cons (see below), this concept has worked for a long time and will continue to work. Nevertheless, there is a new F2F model, which is the central thesis of this book. It is being tested, created, and developed as we speak.

In many of our conversations with industry leaders, investors, entrepreneurs, and innovators, almost nobody believes that F2F is going away. But and this is *a huge but*, almost everyone agrees that there is a new "Exhibitions 2.0" value proposition, and industry stakeholders must learn to adapt their events to this new reality as quickly as possible. We agree that F2F is here to stay, but the overall experience will undoubtedly look quite different in the next decade.

Massive trade shows will still play a role in the future. However, they need to be reinvented in a way that allows buyers and sellers to interact more easily with customized opportunities.

The way that F2F activations are currently developed will evolve into smaller, more sophisticated and productive gatherings allowing buyers and sellers to prepare and select the right meetings, conversations, education, and networking opportunities. As the quality of event connections is critical, one to one (1-2-1) and high-touch models (i.e., Davos for your specific sector) in which curated buyers and sellers can meet based on specific matchmaking criteria represent a high growth event category. They can provide strong ROI that is at least partially measurable to all participants.

We see the F2F moment as critical and unique during the buyer/seller connection. We also see the pre- and post-F2F moments as essential to connect the right people and keep relationships active and relevant as needed throughout the year.

We believe that brands will continue to invest in F2F and value it as a reliable and valuable way to activate and maintain critical connections with customers. Still, the pre/onsite/post-investment budget will change. Also, the Covid experience will make many exhibitors wary of deposits and refund terms. The onsite budget will reflect investments that are easier to implement and measure and generate more substantial ROI. Customers want a better experience, and they will continue to put pressure on all event stakeholders (particularly organizers) to provide a simpler, more efficient customer journey. We see technology as a trustworthy partner in every step of the F2F activation. Brands will be more willing to increase their F2F investments if organizers are engaging innovation regularly (Exhibit 5.3).

Exhibit 5.3 Face to face value proposition—Pros and Cons

Pros	Cons
Proven marketing tool • Highly qualified audience • Attractive cost per lead • Unique buyer-seller connection	Expensive
Range of format options available • Geographic reach global or regional • Formats • Association, corporate or independent	Time consuming
Ability to leverage current and emerging event tech solutions	Challenging to measure outcomes compared to other marketing (ROI)
	Limited seamless integration with year long marketing planning
	Low NPS for sponsors/brands

Virtual

Virtual events are now a couple of decades old. In the early days, however, adoption was lackluster. Some organizers thought that virtual events might replace or damage (or both) F2F events. Others balked at the cost of an unproven concept. And, as we saw in the UBM case study in Chapter 3, for example, participant engagement was relatively marginal during this time for different reasons.

While organizers and users were reluctant to participate in virtual events initially, they are now having a crash course in adoption. Companies like INXPO (now part of Intrado) or ON24 are good examples of some of the original tech solutions in this class, and new players like Hopin or Run The World, among many others, are joining this category with a fresh perspective and technology. As Greg Hitchen, Group CEO of global events company Terrapinn, told us "You can argue that conferences are better in a virtual setting. Virtual is a very interesting opportunity for the future. It is very easy to launch these things. When face-to-face returns, the opportunity to launch virtual will continue."

Virtual events are now a central focus of the events industry. Platforms are changing and improving fast, and we see adoption in B2B and B2C virtual events proliferating. Significant investment in better and more sophisticated software solutions is helping event organizers provide a better and more efficient experience for customers. Previous skeptics have become believers on the realization that the digital audience is potentially bigger than the F2F audience, and this is facilitating ways for brands and attendees to select specific opportunities to engage online.

Nevertheless, virtual events remain a challenge in the current environment. Event organizers need help learning new digital skills in this category, and ventures like Virtual Events Institute, Professional Convention Management Association's (PCMAs) Digital Event Strategist certification program and Event Leadership Institute's Virtual Event and Meeting Management certificate program are facilitating access to content and certification. The direct and indirect monetization of virtual events are still pending. Many for-profit event organizers are still not able to monetize virtual events in a way that can be attractive and sustainable in the long run as a relevant business opportunity in comparison with F2F events. Brands are not ready (yet) to allocate serious investment and budgets because they are still trying to understand the right formula to generate and measure ROI in virtual events.

Despite the obstacles (see Exhibit 5.4), we see clear signals and opportunities for virtual events to allow brands, sponsors, attendees, and speakers to capitalize on the opportunities a massive total addressable market (TAM) presents. The ability to identify, qualify, and nurture relationships and leads in future F2F or hybrid events will be better if event organizers can start cultivating and curating leads as part of their virtual event activities.

Exhibit 5.4 Virtual value proposition—Pros and Cons

Pros	Cons
Low production costs	Hard to monetize • Low attendee fees vs. F2F • Limited sponsor buy-in, so far
Scalable, global reach	Difficulty of driving engagement of participants and sponsors
Interactive tools with audience and sponsors	Lead qualification and conversion rates
Capture valuable data; deploy analytics	
Affordable cost per lead	
Environmentally friendly • Elimination of travel • No waste	
Customizable experience; ability to link to ongoing website content consumption	
Highly effective in some formats (1-2-1, education)	
Long tail 365 content opportunity	

Hybrid

We define a hybrid event as being in-person (F2F) with a digital extension with the opportunity for interaction during the event or directly related to it during the year.

A good example was Apple's special event, announcing the iPhone 11, in September 2019. Content was presented to a live audience at the Steve Jobs Theater in Cupertino, CA and simultaneously livestreamed to a global virtual audience.

The hybrid event idea is powerful, and many smart and sophisticated people in the events and marketing industries (including your co-authors) believe that hybrid events are the future. Organizers wanting to activate their communities through a combination of digital interactions between key buyers and sellers onsite and off-site should pay attention to hybrid events models. It is in the best interests of traditional event organizers to learn from the Covid disruption and maximize digital extensions.

New technologies, coupled with a customer engagement mindset, are facilitating better results and ROI for the hybrid model.

The activation opportunities of hybrid events are virtually limitless. Digital platforms allow organizations to capture and analyze data and customer behavior in many powerful ways. Hybrid event producers can activate events (virtual, hybrid, or just F2F) on an as-needed basis according to geography, buyer-seller needs or hot topics in the sector.

As Kai Hattendorf, CEO at UFI the Global Association of the Exhibition industry told us, "Even the most aggressive advocates for 'digital' events (often called virtual) state that the base for the business relationship is the face-to-face interaction. We have seen that time and again in the past 25+ years. A video call or Zoom conference is no replacement for a real conversation."

The opportunity for event organizers is to fast-track the implementation of digital event elements (that have been in development or are already rolled out), to help deliver an ever better F2F experience during an event. Connecting to contacts and enriching onsite experiences beyond and between the show dates opens the potential to serve industries and customers all year long. As we reflect on the pros and cons table, creating a hybrid model is not easy. Understanding community dynamics and having a very focused and pragmatic approach to each activation is critical. And again, technology is and will be an essential partner for creating 365 engagement with the event as the annual celebration.

Exhibit 5.5 Hybrid value proposition—Pros and Cons

Pros	Cons
Supports F2F activation • Improved participant preparation prevent • Improved follow through	Challenge to win participant time and attention vs alternatives
Extends F2F activation • Audience extension • Extension through the year	Execution challenges • Resource intensive • New culture required • No one-size fits all solution
Improved monetization of brand	Additional expense and potential margin reduction
Limited cost per remote attendee	
Capture valuable data; deploy analytics	
Plan B ready in case of F2F disruption	

Approaching New Event Models with a "Beginner's Mind"

Those who have tried meditation have probably heard about the beginner's mind. In summary, it is a Zen Buddhist concept that refers to adopting an attitude of openness, eagerness, and lack of preconceptions when studying a subject, just as a novice learner would. Organizers that engage this concept in their organizations will have a greater opportunity to create new event models and help customers.

Successful event organizers will need to adopt a permanent "beginner's mind approach."

With more than four thousand event tech solutions (according to the Tracxn Events Tech Sector Landscape Report), identifying the right technology tools can be an intimidating task for event organizers. The secret sauce is giving your buyer and seller community the right platform for creating trust all year long. They should be able to activate any of their specific needs (learning, networking, meetings, product demo, commerce, etc.) at the right time, in the right place through a combination of online, offline, and back to online actions.

Each specific industry, and in many cases geographies, will require organizers to customize event tech and business model solutions as part of the overall event value proposition. In our opinion, there is no shortcut and creating a tech solution that is consistent with the customer journey for each event is critical for success.

Combining the right technologies with the appropriate event model and value proposition will be a critical objective for event organizers.

We are convinced that alternative future models for events will change and evolve faster than ever. And that's exciting news for the industry and all stakeholders.

The Power of Content: Back to the Future

In 1996 Bill Gates famously said, "Content is King." More than a decade later, as part of his Blog World Expo presentation in 2008, Gary Vaynerchuk said, "Content is King, but marketing is Queen and the Queen runs the household."

Successful events are a very effective marketing investment for all stakeholders. We have seen many different ways to generate content for events during the last three decades. Many event organizers acquired media companies to obtain events assets as part of their M&A strategy. In many ways, bringing a community together will require relevant content to provide added value for all members. Event attendees learn from conference content and keep learning visiting the trade show and meeting the right exhibitors offering services or products for these buyers who participate in the event.

As many industry experts shared with us as part of our research for this book, it seems that we are witnessing "Back to the Future" with the growing recognition of the importance of content. It is a critical attracting force for attendees element as part of the digital and face-to-face engagement at events.

Event organizers will need to rethink how they want to generate their content and invest in the internal talent for content development, or partner with existing content providers or acquire them to build future business models for their communities. Digital content can now have a greater impact on the F2F event experience, and increase community engagement during the rest of the year. Capturing your audience's commitment and time will become a unique differentiation for long-term success and sustainable growth for successful events.

From Platforms to Potential B2B Marketplaces: Opportunities and Challenges for the Events Industry

For many years now, event organizers have been attempting to facilitate digital engagement and connections for their community members before and after the event. Improving their event websites and generating content are both essential, but not enough.

Creating year-round digital platforms where communities can access product information, curated content, education, lead generation, and networking can improve the event value proposition and customer outcomes. They can also generate significant data, which organizers can use to extract commitment to the event brand.

We define a B2B marketplace as a digital platform that includes commerce and enables buyers and sellers to connect. Joor, Faire, and NuORDER are some examples of successful B2B marketplaces helping their buyers and sellers to transact online.

Owners can monetize B2B digital platforms through advertising, memberships, lead generation, transaction fees, and many alternative options.

The concept of B2B Marketplaces is also a couple of decades old. Vertical Net and Ariba were original pioneers of the idea in the late '90s. For many years, B2B marketplaces were not successful; Platform providers took considerable time, money, and resources to understand the way that B2B buyers and sellers could interact in the digital world versus offline.

Some event organizers started offering digital platforms solutions years ago. Examples include MOM, which is part of Maison and Objet, a Reed France event and Informa Market's Fashion marketplace. Several pure digital players are partnering with event organizers: NuORDER with Informa, Alibaba with the China Council for the Promotion of International Trade (CCPIT) and Tencent with Canton Fair and many more coming soon.

CASE STUDY
INFORMA MARKETS FASHION AND NUORDER PARTNERSHIP: AN ALL-YEAR, END-TO-END SOLUTION FOR CUSTOMERS

Summary

Informa Markets Fashion joined forces with specialized fashion online marketplace NuORDER to provide year-round commerce and engagement for buyers and sellers.

Context

In May 2020, in the midst of the Covid crisis, Informa unveiled a partnership with B2B fashion online marketplace NuORDER. Year-round features include a digital catalogue, interactive virtual rooms, and an online payment and ordering system.

One month later, Informa had to cancel its in-person events due to Covid. The partnership allowed the marketplace to remain.

Objectives of the Partnership

- **Both parties benefit from the partnership.** The alliance permits Informa to provide customers with year-round digital offerings that complement their live shows and extend the visibility of events from days to weeks, and ultimately to 365 days a year. NuORDER is able to enhance its offerings with live experiences and bring new customers to the platform. Both parties participate in revenues.
- **Basis for partnership**

Shared vision

The partners share the same vision and see mutual benefits in delivering physical and digital services to their customers. They acknowledge the importance of both channels.

> *"We shared the exact same vision that physical shows and meeting people face-to-face will remain very important but could be improved by having a digital platform that runs alongside it all year round."* Co-Founder & Co-CEO, NuORDER

Common expertise and complementary skills

Informa Markets Fashion and NuORDER both have in-depth knowledge of the fashion industry, each with an established reputation for tailored retailer and fashion brand offerings.

> *"NuORDER is fashion-focused and it was a perfect fit for our portfolio. There was a quick understanding, they already had relationships with the brands, with retailers. For us it was a match made in heaven."* Fashion Portfolio President, Informa Markets

With mutual respect for each other's skill set, both sought to partner with best-in-class players.

"We see digital and live events as totally complementary to each other. We looked at a couple of different companies and NuORDER had the perfect capability we were looking for." Fashion Portfolio President, Informa Markets

"We knew that Informa has the expertise in doing the sales of the show and its marketing. We will not interfere with them on that." Co-Founder & Co-CEO, NuORDER

Lessons Learned

It is still too early to tell if B2B marketplaces and events are perfect bedfellows in practice, as well as in theory, but there are some emerging lessons.

Finding the right partner with an end-to-end solution for customers

Culture fit, strategic alignment and the common ground of genuine complementary skills are key elements ensuring the success of the partnership.

"It's essential to focus on categories. You need specific features for each category and you need to have a nomenclature knowledge of these categories. At the end of the day, especially in B2B Marketplaces, you really do need to have the knowledge of each industry." Co-Founder & Co-CEO, NuORDER

Learning from others versus developing internally

Best-of breed-capabilities and skills may best be found through partnering as opposed to developing them in-house. A partnership allows both sides to leverage their respective experience and relationships.

> *"Physical shows and digital are different skillsets. There's only a couple of things you can do very well. Let's just focus on what we are good at and then bring the best of the best where we want to provide that experience to our customers."* Co-Founder & Co-CEO, NuORDER

Right timing

The collaboration coincided with the adoption of online marketplaces by industry professionals. The trend started in the late 2010s, but the Covid crisis accelerated it.

> *"It's been a tipping point in the last two years. Adoption of online marketplaces by fashion brands and retailers increased, and all of a sudden we had enough buyers and sellers to match both sides of the equation."* Co-Founder & Co-CEO, NuORDER

Alternative Options for Building a Digital Platform or Marketplace

The idea of helping B2B buyers and sellers connect all year long through a digital platform and ideally complement the F2F event experience certainly makes a lot of sense for some industries such as retail.

It's certainly not an easy task and will require serious investment and commitment from stakeholders along with new digital management skills. We can think of three alternative options for event organizers to interact with B2B platforms or marketplaces:

- First, create solutions in-house, with existing technology, marketing tools and management teams

- Second, license existing Software-as-a-Service (SaaS) solutions to creating the B2B platform and focus on the marketing part of the business to add value for events communities
- Third, partner with a B2B marketplace established in a vertical. In this collaboration, each party plays to its strengths, and the event organizer keeps 100 percent of its focus on its events

There is another option as well, which is simply to ignore this concept and think that having a digital platform doesn't make any sense and will never be needed to support an event. Good luck with this one if this is your decision ☺.

Creating a platform from scratch with a tech and marketing team is a brave decision. Some prominent organizers are experimenting with this option. Easyfairs is an example of a success story but time will tell how many others can create successful and sustainable platforms.

Stephan Forseilles, head of technology and digital transformation at Easyfairs, shared his own ideas about creating their own platform B2B Marketplace.

> "It only works under certain circumstances. I'd say the minimum set of pre-requisites are:
>
> - A completely centralized tech stack allowing for common development/deployment/training across all events and geographies. Only this allows the economies of scale that make it sustainable.
> - A common strategy on all tech/digital aspects: CIO, CTO and CDO must speak in ONE voice. If the CMO can tag along it's even better.
> - Laser-like focus, commitment and trust from the CEO and board to allow for long-term investments without a completely defined business case. That's especially true for areas like A.I. that require months, sometimes years of work before yielding tangible results."

Using existing SaaS solutions such as Balluun or Mirakl, which are helping event organizers, associations, and media companies create B2B digital platforms, is another way to go. With this option, organizers are customizing the vendor's software based on their industry-specific needs.

Finally, if an industry already has one or more successful B2B digital platforms or marketplaces, organizers can consider partnering with the best option available. Before doing so, we suggest careful analysis of ways to provide value to the community and, in parallel, protect intellectual property (IP) assets such as databases and customer relationships. If the partnership collapses, collaboration (and potentially competition at a future point) with well-established B2B marketplaces can be complex.

The critical skills for organizing events versus creating digital platforms are dramatically different. Bringing these skills on board and getting everyone to work together effectively is one of the most important challenges to adopting future event models. We look at this in greater detail in Chapter 9. Successful future event models will have a combination of digital and F2F interactions for buyers and sellers to facilitate commerce and generate sustainable trust in their communities.

Aaron Levant, Founder of Ntwrk, a sort of "QVC for the Gen Z generation," raised money from LiveNation, Footlocker, Drake, Jimmy Lovine, Warner Brothers, and Arnold Schwarzenegger, among other strategic investors and celebrities. He founded the Agenda trade show and sold it to Reed Exhibitions before launching Ntwrk and continues to participate in the events industry as an investor.

Aaron shared some great feedback and ideas with us about the intersection of events, digital platforms, and the customer experience with alternative event models.

"Ntwrk was inspired by events. After selling Agenda, my idea was to start consumer-related ventures seeing the Direct to Consumer trend.

- Building digital communities is tough, expensive, and super competitive. Ntwrk was created thinking about an experience that combines digital experience and physical activation, including drop shipping on B2C events controlling customer experience as a critical priority. That's the idea with Ntwrk, and, we will activate digital events in July 2020 and move to real events in the future.
- Digital platforms like Ntwrk linked to physical events in the future will capture data. They will be able to activate live events and monetize through tickets, special offers with credit card companies, revenue sharing, etc. instead of the traditional trade show monetization model."

Connecting Modern Buyers and Sellers

We believe that modern buyers and sellers will continue to demand better and more efficient events experiences. We also think events organizers are finally realizing that these demands are simply not going away. It's a matter of survival for events themselves to understand and engage with new innovative business models to meet those demands.

In many different parts, case studies, and messages in this book, we share concrete examples and ideas on ways to leverage tech and new models as part of any event value proposition. Nevertheless, we must emphasize the complexity of changing and blending legacy events into the new world.

Many events have been successful for many years or decades. They have enjoyed growth and profits along the road. For successful events, adjusting to future events models and incorporating tech as part of the offering will be both challenging and complicated.

Events teams with such longevity are great operators; they understand logistics, hospitality, sales, and marketing plans for their shows exceptionally well. Still, they don't understand how to extend their products into the digital world.

As Julius Solaris, Founder of EventMB mentioned during our conversation:

> "Seismic change in the meeting planner's industry and the challenges that we were discussing for the last 20–30 years will happen in a couple of years. Security, insurance, and the overall nature of events will be adjusted. It's no longer about great food & beverage or having a nice room anymore. It's about great content and networking opportunities."

Traditional organizers are not digital community or digital marketing experts. They are certainly not data engineers or software coders who can develop software solutions quickly and effectively. We don't think that this is a death sentence for these organizations, but it is a serious challenge.

We are currently seeing a profound transformation in legacy event organizers. They are making a genuine effort to innovate and adapt their events. We also recognize that prominent organizers will continue to acquire smaller entrepreneurial events and teams to foster innovation inside their organizations.

These are still the early days (or the Wild West days as we say) for the F2F transformation. We are identifying new models and formats faster than ever, but we are also learning that changing hundreds of years of history is neither easy nor fast.

We are living through a fantastic time for innovation and new business models in the events industry. Talented and hardworking entrepreneurs and corporations are building incredible products and reinventing the way events will continue to serve industries and fans for decades to come.

Conclusions

- Face to Face will continue to be a central and critical part of the B2B marketing value proposition, but it is becoming decreasingly isolated from other forms of engagement.
- Technology will play a strategic role in helping stakeholders define, set, and measure KPIs and ROI for the events category.
- We are still in the infancy of identifying definitive new events models. There will be many, not just one!
- "The genie is out of the bottle" with enforced choices post-Covid. Virtual and hybrid event models are firmly on the map.

Chapter 6

Event Tech

The Last Ten Years and the Next Ten Years.
Constraints and Drivers

> "Nothing diminishes anxiety better than action."
> Walter Anderson

In the last chapter, we discussed reinventing the events value proposition and engaging with innovation, new technologies, and business models. Now, let's get a bit more granular and look at what we have learned from event technologies in the past and figure out which opportunities we could capitalize on in the future.

For many marketers and event organizers, event tech engagement has been a source of anxiety for years. Some people are simply in denial, thinking that tech will never affect the industry. Others have regular anxiety attacks thinking that tech will kill their businesses.

Some act. We are pretty sure that readers of this book fall into the doer category. But let's be honest, there are significant challenges for event owners attempting to coax their customers into adopting technology.

There are multiple friction layers for event tech adoption. Organizers must select the right tech partners. Technology providers must integrate their technologies in a way that benefits customers (exhibitors, attendees, speakers, etc.) and other suppliers (general contractors, venues, etc.). Exhibitors and attendees have to engage with event tech to maximize opportunities. Organizers have to remove each friction layer (from organizer to tech provider to exhibitor to attendee) before they can expect continued and sustainable success.

It is very easy for event tech companies to complain about organizers or vice versa. It's also very easy for exhibitors (sellers) to complain about a lack of engagement from attendees (buyers). Event organizers will usually complain about event tech and mention that they have over-promised and under-delivered for years. Many organizers are also concerned by the fact that some event tech companies are small startups with no substantial funding and resources and they are not ready to support their specific security and scalability needs.

On the other hand, event tech owners will usually complain about lack of engagement and investment levels from event organizers and about their limited technological knowledge. The phrase that we keep hearing is about dinosaurs trying to survive the new world.

But all stakeholders have to make a conscious effort at collaboration to generate concrete results. Sounds complicated? It is. Sounds impossible? Not at all, and the industry is moving in the right direction.

This concept is already working in many industries. We see great examples in industries like FinTech, TravelTech, or HealthTech, where many different stakeholders are working together to maximize collaboration and partnership opportunities. For example, a TravelTech company such as Booking.com has to partner with hotels, airlines, transportation companies, service providers, and many other offline and online partners to generate a fantastic user experience for its customers.

Successful event tech companies are doing the same. They are listening to their customers and working with many different partnerships and integrations (venues, service providers, exhibitors, attendees, and of course, organizers) to provide a consistent and productive customer experience for everyone.

Now, more than ever, the events industry will need collaboration and partnerships to succeed. We believe that event tech companies will play a significant role in activating many of these partnerships leading to unprecedented innovation over the next decade. But event organizers must have an open mind for creating productive partnerships that will benefit all stakeholders. We will look again at this topic in greater detail in Chapter 8.

Technology, even in the events industry, is beginning to evolve very quickly. Event tech was born in the 1970s or even before then if audio visual breakthroughs are placed into the mix. And, incremental technologies and solutions have consistently emerged every decade (registration, lead generation, event management software, etc.)

Post-internet, however, the events industry experienced a significant acceleration in technology development with dozens of tech categories mushrooming into existence for all event stakeholders. The next decade will be unlike any we have seen before. It already feels as if the afterburners have been turned on.

Software Is Eating the World. And What about Events?

The famous phrase from Mark Andreesen, "Software is eating the world," is almost ten years old, but it is more relevant than ever. It's crazy to think that products and services such as the iPhone, Kindle, Uber, Airbnb, Android, or Spotify didn't exist in 2006. Because software has bloomed, the way participants can interact with event content has also evolved. In the old days, watching Bill Gates present live at Comdex was a once in a lifetime opportunity. Today, almost all content is available online sooner or later, and our relationship with content and educational opportunities at events has changed dramatically.

We have also seen technology change the way we promote our events (from brochures to digital marketing), how we connect at events (from business cards to lead retrieval to AI matchmaking-generated meetings), the list goes on and on. These technologies affect the way event organizers, associations, exhibitors, venues, vendors, attendees, and speakers interact with real-life event experiences.

In our 2017 book, *The Face of Digital,* my (Marco's) co-author Jay Weintraub (you can read more about Jay and his views about how to win in the InsureTech case study) and I said, "The face-to-face industry is currently in the midst of an identity crisis. As with all crises, it brings the opportunity to emerge stronger and more unified."

Almost four years later, the identity crisis is different. Denzil and I think we will now see ten or twenty years of innovation in only a couple of years.

It Is Not Love that Unites Us but Fear

In his beautiful poem "Buenos Aires," the fantastic Jorge Luis Borges said, "It is not love that unites us but fear." Event professionals have been united by fear, or more accurately terror, with Covid, seeing billions of dollars in losses accompanying uncertainty about the length and pain of the wait for a "new normal."

We need to reshuffle event tech and innovation priorities based on this new reality and opportunity. Some of the technologies described only a few years ago are now obsolete or have transitioned into new product categories. A good example is mobile apps. This was a significant category in the early and mid-2000s, but it became part of suite software solutions when organizers demanded more integration between their event tech solutions.

Recently, we saw rampant M&A activity in the event tech world. Cvent purchased SocialTables and DoubleDutch. Aventri acquired etouches, Loopd, and ITN International, and there are many more examples. We also see exciting growth in new categories, like virtual event platforms (Hopin, Intrado, On24, etc.) and AI matchmaking (Grip, SwapCard, Brella), creating significant opportunities for their customers to improve engagement and value for events customers.

Many failed event tech startups were simply unable to survive the long sales cycles, complex client requirements, and slow user adoption. Other startups though are experiencing steady growth because they are helping event owners to reinvent their value proposition and adjusting to virtual and hybrid solutions.

An interesting example is Grip, an AI matchmaking solution based in London. Tim Groot, Founder and CEO told us,

> "Grip is about establishing intelligent business interactions, and that's what the organizers of the future should be doing—connecting markets all year round in virtual, hybrid, and in-person event experiences. Organizers should leverage their brands, reach, and market position as a neutral player to monetize connections within those networks. Traditionally, this was done by charging per square meter. However, much more innovative models are possible, such as charging per meeting, lead, or 'view' as B2B marketers are used to in online advertising platforms such as Facebook and Google."

Another tech category that has been poised to be the next big thing for a while is Augmented Reality/Virtual Reality/Mixed Reality (AR/VR/MR).

We believe that these technologies could and should help the way that brands educate customers and showcase products faster and more efficiently than ever, not only at their stores but also at in-person events. Until now, very few relevant players have grown in this space. Content generation for AR/VR/MR is still expensive and difficult to execute for many brands. This situation is changing with companies like Los Angeles-based VNTANA, which develops affordable and scalable 3D product solutions.

We also see AR/VR-related startups like Teeoh, Gathr, and YouCan facilitating B2B activations and B2C-oriented solutions like virtual concert creator Wave gaining significant traction.

Other tech categories are more evergreen. For example, registration and ticketing continue to attract significant investment and are also the targets of significant M&A activity.

Investor Views

There are mixed feelings among investors about the event tech category. Most recognize the massive Total Addressable Market (TAM) and economic impact opportunity ($2.5+ trillion of dollars based on the events industry council report) with low tech adoption. The investment community is poised for innovation acceleration. Because these are attractive attributes for investors and entrepreneurs, event tech companies will continue to attract quality talent, and we can expect to see creative startups joining the industry.

But the events industry still has very few successful event tech Unicorns. Tracxn reports a couple more Soonicorns may join Eventbrite and Cvent, including Bizzabo, Certain, Convene, and Eved. Hopin is the newest unicorn (actually a double unicorn) in the event tech category with a $2.125 Billion valuation after their Series B funding announcement in November of 2020. But scaling fast has significant challenges in a highly fragmented industry that is slow to adopt. Nevertheless, billions of dollars from smart venture capital and private equity investors are coming into event tech, and thousands of event tech startups are trying to solve problems and generate new business models.

Identifying which technologies are going to be transformational for the in-person events industry is not an easy task.

When we talked with event tech founders like Eran Ben-Shushan, co-Founder and CEO at Bizzabo, about the lack of unicorns, he answered that we are still in the early days. Nevertheless, being a non-sexy, old-school industry makes it more difficult to raise big capital and rapidly scale.

As we discussed in Chapter 5, future event models will motivate organizers, sponsors, and attendees to engage with technology as part of the customer journey. The incremental use of event tech and accelerated growth of many startups will encourage new investors to capitalize talented entrepreneurs building the next generation of potential event tech unicorns.

As you can see in the following graphic (Exhibit 6.1) these are the most relevant event tech areas from an investment/fundraising perspective.

Virtual Events 2.0

Virtual events technologies made a comeback due to Covid. Thousands of events cancellations created the need for alternate solutions to keep event communities together. Virtual events were the available short-term solution for this problem. Now, this time round, virtual events technologies are different from those of the early 2000s. The customer mindset for engaging with this technology and the value proposition offered by organizers is way different than twenty plus years ago.

As Tim Groot from Grip mentioned,

> "Virtual events are going to have a profound impact on the event technology category. The main reason is that virtual event platforms have a price point that is several times higher than any other event technology product such as event registration, event management, event matchmaking or event apps.

Exhibit 6.1 Event tech market map

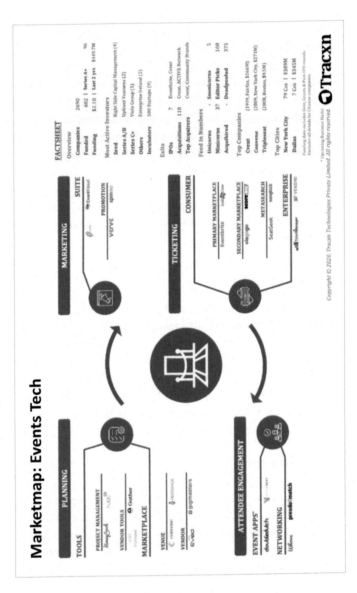

Source Tracxn event tech report.

As a result, Virtual event platforms are going to be able to have larger technology teams and more powerful sales and marketing, which will overshadow all other event technology segments.

Event Technology will, therefore, grow massively as a category attracting more funding, acquisitions and innovation that is created on top of these virtual event platforms that will consolidate other individual products into a single product suite. They might also create their own app exchanges such as Salesforce has done, enabling third-party developers to create deep integrations with their product resulting in organizers being even more deeply tied in with those platforms."

Virtual events will need to focus on new ways to provide unique content, learning, networking and product/service exposure to buyers in a way no other channel does. They will need to create new and compelling customer experiences and reinvent the way that people, products, and companies connect.

The combination of better and more affordable technologies and a much bigger and more educated customer base will allow virtual events 2.0 to play a more significant role and gain a large market share in the industry.

Finally, virtual events are no longer isolated from F2F. Investing in virtual events that have a broader strategy and integrate with other event activations will deliver incremental benefits and return on investment for all participants.

Understanding Event Tech Categories

Since we are covering many different event categories in our book, we will focus on technologies that could be used in different types of events without going too geeky into our analysis.

We will also discuss how some software and hardware solutions that are currently used in other verticals like retail, hospitality, travel, or logistics could have concrete benefits for events stakeholders. Based on different event activations and opportunities, from B2B to B2C experiences, event organizers can learn from other industries and take shortcuts to leverage some of those same tech opportunities for their events.

We have regular conversations with venture capital and private equity investors on expansion opportunities in their portfolios of adjacent event and event technology verticals, such as sports, music festivals, corporate events, or tradeshows. But we also see retail or travel tech solutions that could and should play a role. For example, hyper geo-location technologies or indoor sensors help shopping malls track visitors. The same tech could be used in exhibition halls. Similarly, there are tremendous opportunities for founders who are building technologies to improve the buyer–seller experience. Smart event organizers are already adopting these technologies faster than ever before.

We will cover specific case studies sharing best practices and successful implementations, trying to spark some ideas and opportunities with our readers about ways to experiment with their own goals and needs regardless of your event role or responsibility.

Most likely, we will repeat a simple but powerful concept all over our book when we discuss innovation. Innovation will not only rely on engaging specific technologies. Real and impactful innovation happens when all stakeholders engage with technology and change their goals and expectations of a live-event experience.

Consumer behavior is finally changing, and that's a complicated thing. Online platforms are training billions of future virtual and hybrid events stakeholders faster than ever. And this too is creating a huge market opportunity for the events industry.

Event Tech Is Augmenting TAM—the Events Industry TAM

Technology is creating a massive new audience for the events industry. Every event organizer should be interested in developing and understanding the technologies that maximize user engagement and value for their communities. Eran from Bizzabo, one of the leading corporate event operating systems, has a long and deep history with event tech, and has particular views on future opportunities for corporate events organizers. Some of his customers are corporations that produce events for their customers that range from small to massive, working hard to facilitate more and better experiences in their audiences.

Eran thinks that technology for events will continue to improve

- "If tech is engaged in the right way by customers. Tech will augment the number of delegates, attendees, globally for organizers exponentially. Some known examples are Microsoft building from 6k people in Seattle into 250k people globally and Hubspot from 20k into 100k."
- "Physical events will be better than ever in the future, and the level of efficiencies will increase exponentially."

By combining virtual, hybrid, and F2F events and activations, organizers will be able to augment their TAM, capitalize on new revenue opportunities, and provide incremental benefits to their communities.

Let's take a look into some specific event tech categories and examples.

Event Tech Main Categories and Case Studies

Event tech is broad and diverse, and there are many ways to categorize it. If we use investment as a key parameter, registration and ticketing are by far the largest and most relevant category. Event tech can also be differentiated by solutions such as event marketing or by event formats, such as virtual, hybrid, conference, or exhibition. Categories like B2B, B2C, and entertainment, describe technologies based on participant needs.

The types of event organizers, corporate event organizers, associations (which also organize many events as a critical revenue source), professional meeting planners, and so on can dictate event technology categorization. Events can also differ across industries. Tech events are different from travel, food, or furniture events and some technologies may be unique to those verticals. We also need to think of geographies; for example, facial recognition is standard in Asia for registration but not elsewhere.

Event organizers need to focus on event tech priorities that are relevant for multiple stakeholders in their communities. Do less, better. This is a fundamental concept when you are adding tech layers into your event experience. Trying to activate too many event technologies in parallel is usually a recipe for disaster, while allocating enough resources and investments to educate stakeholders on the right way to engage with each solution is a best practice.

Adam Parry is the co-founder and editor of the event industry's global online magazine, *Event Industry News*. www.eventindustrynews. com. He also co-founded Event Tech Live, which is The World's Leading Event Technology Expo, the only show dedicated to event technology. Adam shared his thoughts with us on event tech categories of the future. The highlights of our conversation included comments on ROI, analytics, and digital revenues.

- "Some of the exciting event tech categories are focused on analyzing return of investment (ROI) measurement, mainly now since hybrid and virtual will increase data collection."
- "Analytics as part of helping event organizers to understand ways to use their data supporting all events stakeholders."
- "Digital revenues and ad spend will continue to evolve into a relevant category for organizers capturing exhibitors'

budgets that could be allocated into an integrated marketing approach with the overall event experience, and Digital marketing technologies will increase this opportunity."

We could go deeper into each of these categories, but it's not our priority for this book. What we want to share with you are some critical messages on why event tech is relevant for the future of events and where smart and successful event organizers should focus their resources.

Exhibit 6.2 sets out the major event tech categories.

Exhibit 6.2   Major event tech categories

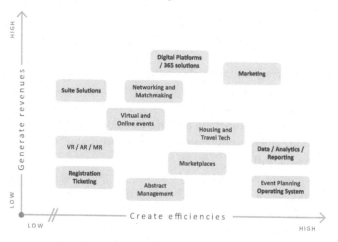

Note: Numerous smaller categories such as events discovery, venues, speaker recruitment, heatmaps, and indoor location, bots, calendaring, etc. not included

Here is some more detail on each of the major categories.

1. **Suite Solutions** (Cvent, Aventri, Bizzabo)
   Companies providing different integrated suites of software solutions to manage the entire event cycle.

2. **Digital Platforms/365 Solutions** *(Balluun, Mirakl, Uppler)*
   Companies providing yearlong software as service solutions to manage digital platforms and marketplaces.

3. **Event Planning and Operating System** *(Hubb, Lennd, HoneyBook)*
   Companies focused on software solutions related to manage activities related to event planning processes.

4. **Marketplaces** (venues, vendors, industries) *(Convene, Eved)*
   B2B marketplaces connecting buyers and sellers in different event related areas or specific event related industries.

5. **Marketing** *(Feathr, EventCloud, Gleanin)*
   Software solutions used to promote marketing efforts and promote attendees and exhibitors/sponsors engagement and participation. SEO, SEM, Retargeting, Email, Social media campaigns are included in this category.

6. **Registration and Ticketing** (B2B, B2C, Marketplace, Secondary Marketplace, Metasearch) *(Eventbrite, Ticketmaster, SeatGeek)*
   Technology (hardware and software) helping organizers to register and check in attendees to their events, including buying tickets, RSPV, guest lists, etc.

7. **Attendee Networking and Matchmaking** (audience interaction, mobile apps, matchmaking, networking) *(Grip, Brella, SwapCard)*
   Software powered by AI focused on providing networking, qualified leads, and matchmaking opportunities and meetings between buyers and sellers.

8. **Virtual and Online Events** *(Hopin, Bizzabo, HeySummit)*
   Software platforms focused on hosting online and virtual events (including live and on demand).

9. **VR/AR/MR** *(Helios, Spark AR)*
   Hardware and software solutions incorporating virtual, augmented, or mixed reality into in-person events experiences.

10. **Abstract Management** *(Cadmium, Hubb, Confex)*
    Software as service solutions for call-for-papers process by allowing the submission, review, and selection of session content and planning.

11. **Housing and Travel Tech related to in-person events** (*OnPeak, PassKey, Resiada*)
    Software solutions helping organizers to support their attendees and exhibitors/sponsors housing needs. This category includes transportation, hotels, and related services.

12. **Data, Analytics, Reporting**
    Software solutions helping event organizers for data aggregation and analysis for different use cases and reporting and insights to event stakeholders.

Other categories

There is long list of other categories that are either peripheral or nascent. They include Association management solutions, Events discovery, Venue discovery and selection, Speaker recruitment, Crowdfunding for events, heatmaps and indoor location sensors, bots, calendaring/scheduling, and many more.

Integration

Significant events require at least ten and sometimes as many as twenty different technologies. While some event tech companies are offering turnkey solutions, sophisticated organizers still want to integrate best in class technologies to facilitate a great user experience.

Integration is desirable but very difficult to execute. Freeman created its own integrations platform (Fuzion), and there are others, including Blendrio and Tray.io, plus more prominent players that are not event focused, such as Zapier or Mulesoft, which Salesforce acquired in 2018 for $6.5 billion. Bob Priest Heck, CEO at Freeman told us,

> "Freeman started investing in digital technology years ago not because we knew a pandemic was coming, but because we knew digital enhancements make every event better, more relevant and more personal. Fuzion is the platform that makes

it easier to integrate all the amazing event technology and the data they generate. The data reveal insights that allow us to design highly contextualized event experiences—better experiences— in person or virtually. That's the metric that matters, right?"

The Event Is Over. And Now?

It has been a continuing challenge for event tech to maintain its relevance when the show is over. We talked about this in *The Face of Digital*.

The difficulty lies in the fact that event participants tend to move on to the next thing after the event concludes, and existing tech tools do not help to keep the conversation going. Nevertheless, there is hope, particularly where B2B platforms and marketplaces are concerned. We cover this topic in detail in different parts of our book.

A Very Fragmented Market

There are more than four thousand event tech companies. Use cases are too fragmented, and the fact that events can represent multiple industries, geographies, and customers are creating many more use cases regularly.

In many cases, a high level of tech customization is required. This is not a good thing for most software companies since they need to customize their software for specific use cases instead of being able to scale a SaaS solution to millions of customers with similar needs.

Eran from Bizzabo says,

"The consolidation of tools is essential for our customers. You need to keep it simple. Integration and data are critical. Also, empathizing with your customers is the baseline for building a solution that has a high product-market fit. Event planning involves extremely high levels of complexity and anxiety. Understanding that, at the deepest levels, is inherent in building the right technology and products for the events market."

We have mentioned the critical need for strategic partnerships between event technology companies, organizers, and their customers (exhibitors and attendees). But creating these partnerships takes time.

Finding the right solutions and partners requires bravery and an investment of time, money, and energy. Patience, humility, and persistence will also go a long way. There are no magic tricks. There are only open and transparent conversations with stakeholders, colleagues, and team members about engaging with technology regularly to find ways to add value to the event ecosystem. The good news is customers want innovation and they are ready to use tools that make their event experiences more productive and enjoyable.

We believe that if you are brave enough to be reading this book, you are going in the right direction. This is quite intimidating stuff, and for many people reading about technology, transformation and the future are out of their comfort zone. But let's be honest, if you are not ready to move out of your comfort zone in this industry, you should probably look for a new career path.

If you are ready to keep moving, let's jump into Chapter 7 and discuss some of our ideas about the future of the events industry.

Conclusions

- Change in event tech will be constant and quick during the next ten years.
- More and better talent, investment, and adoption will accelerate event tech companies' growth.
- Successful event organizers will adjust their value proposition to include tech as a critical part of their customer journey.

- We are still in the early days of event tech and we will see a rapid evolution of the major categories. As gatekeepers, event organizers, venues, and suppliers are finally taking tech seriously and investing, learning, and engaging with tech solutions.
- Other stakeholders (attendees, exhibitors, and sponsors) are ready to engage with tech.

Chapter 7

The Online-Offline-Online Thesis

"You Must Unlearn What You Have Learned."
Yoda in Episode V, *The Empire Strikes Back.*

Well, now that we have examined some of the history of the events industry, why events are changing, some potential future events business models, and the way that technology will play a vital role into the future, we would like to share with you, our beloved and courageous reader, our OOO (Online-Offline-Online) thesis.

But, before we get started, we want to repeat the phrase Yoda uttered when he was training young Luke Skywalker, "You must unlearn what you have learned."

If you are a corporate executive, marketing professional, event organizer, customer or attendees, you must rethink (and unlearn) the way that you have interacted with events until now. Tech and consumer behavior changes are transforming many industries. We already pointed out examples in media and travel, and there are more we have not mentioned.

Professional and sophisticated event organizers provide plenty of value in brand recognition, leads, networking, and education, and they will continue to provide these benefits to all participants.

Nevertheless, we believe that future events, like communities, will need to be relevant and active all year long.

We think that an essential part of this concept is "leads as a service" (LaaS).

Brands/sellers should be able to activate, qualify, and convert leads regularly as part of their events investment all year round. LaaS is a new revenue model for event organizers, which includes annual subscriptions and tiered memberships in a year-round online community. Furthermore, LaaS is not only about incremental revenue opportunities for organizers. It's about something profoundly deeper—providing more and better interactions with customers and helping them to benefit from being part of the community.

LaaS substantially enhances the lead-delivery part of the event. Brand recognition, networking, and education, which are very different value propositions for event customers will remain part of the event and continue to generate significant revenue opportunities for organizers.

From 3 to 365 Days

Online or offline, buyers and sellers, fans, teams, and celebrities want to be free to connect, learn, and share relevant information easily and all the time. Event organizers must create a connected and productive experience for them (Exhibit 7.1).

Exhibit 7.1 The 3 to 365 concept

	The past	Today	Tomorrow
What marketers buy	Floor space	Space plus some additional services such as education	Lead gen platform charged per lead (LaaS) Brand building and other content services including education
Space sales	100%	80%	< 50%
Lead qualification	Large horizontal audience	Qualified audience	Highly qualified and engaged audience
Duration	3 days	3 days plus some extension	365

Development of event technology, RoI measurement, microtargeting, data capture and analytics

In real life, in-person meetings are a critical tool for establishing trust with new customers and for maintain it. Online connections are critical for maintaining trust and rapport.

The event activation moment is like a feast or celebration where months of hard work finally allow buyers and sellers, fans, celebrities, or athletes to connect face to face. But what about the time before and after the event? Event organizers can own that connection space too.

New technologies and digital platforms enable that celebration and those connections and experiences in ways that we would never have imagined before. The combination of online and offline community activations help stakeholders stay connected and maximize business opportunities efficiently.

Do We Need to Do This in Person, or Is Online Just Fine?

We think that events as an industry will see similar levels of transformation as some other industries. Telehealth has revolutionized healthcare and remote work technologies have completely changed work.

As Sheryl Sandberg (Facebook COO) stated in a Bloomberg Technology interview in 2020, "This year, we will learn what has to be done in person." Remote work is the new work and large corporations are rethinking what needs to be done face to face and could be accomplished online. Well, do you think that this "simple concept" could affect the events industry? We believe so.

There are different views on this concept. Many successful leaders including Netflix CEO and Co-Founder Reed Hasting are not strong supporters of working from home. They have signaled this clearly in various articles, for example saying "Not being able to get together in person, particularly internationally, is a pure negative," when asked about the benefits of working from home and the desire to have employees back at the office as soon as possible. Other strong and successful leaders like Jack Dorsey, Co-Founder and CEO at Twitter and Square said "We want employees to be able to work where they feel most creative and productive," after announcing that employees of both companies could work from home "forever."

As an event organizer, you will need to rethink when customers need to attend the in-person event and when it is more effective for them to participate from the comfort of their home or office.

Part of our OOO thesis considers that the future of events is no longer only face to face or strictly online. It's both, in parallel and all year long. Each industry will have different specific needs for in-person events in the future and event organizers will need to customize their events value proposition based on the specific industry dynamics online, offline, and online again during the whole annual cycle.

We are starting to see professional sports leagues, for example, deliver unique and personalized online experiences at NBA or NFL games to fans seated in their premium stadium seats. Music artists are performing in person to premium fans who are willing to pay and streaming the performances to a completely different audience. A virtual concert of K-Pop superstars BTS attracted 756,600 concurrent viewers from 107 regions, grossing $20m and expanding its fan club by 10,000.

Corporate Events Ideas and Models

Corporate events and trade shows are experimenting with OOO, in 2020, companies like Apple and Snap introduced a completely new approach for their corporate events. They learned new and creative ways to engage with their global audiences through virtual events at a very competitive cost per delegate.

Some corporate event organizers, such Nicola Kastner, vice president and global head of event marketing strategy at SAP do not understand why it has taken so long to adopt strategies like OOO. "I've being saying for years that the events industry is ready for disruption and as a tech company, we see disruption happening every day in multiple industries. We are sophisticated tech consumers in our daily life, but it seems that we check expectations at the door when we attend a B2B event and seem to be OK having a disconnected experience," she says.

This is precisely what our OOO thesis helps to address. If event organizers think like community catalysts and not food, beverage, and logistics operators, or high-powered sales machines, they can orchestrate continuous, creative, and connected experiences every day of the year.

Live experiences at events are a critical part of OOO, and we firmly believe that replacing the human connection, and experience with tech is almost impossible.

The VP Global Marketing at one of the world's largest tech firms told us during our conversation "Events still have a long way to go in terms of tech. Some events are still very disconnected with tech like music or sports, and some events like trade shows are more connected."

Technology Helping Content, Networking, and Commerce at In-Person Events

The combination of technologies focused on content, networking, and commerce will be the inevitable path for future B2B communities. Face to face can no longer be isolated or disconnected from the rest of the marketing stack. Exhibit 7.2 sets out our OOO thesis—Online–Offline–Online

Exhibit 7.2 Online–offline–online

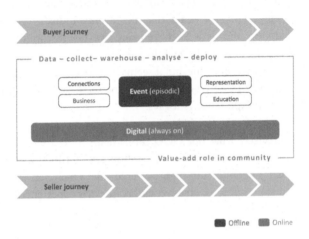

Industry ecosystem

As we are discussing in case studies and chapters throughout this book, the skills of event organizer team members will need to change dramatically.

Kerry Gumas, founder and former CEO of Questex, a leading B2B media and event organizer, envisions how technology will empower the next iteration of community (not just event) experiences. "A new business model is being created now and should be SaaS oriented with yearlong solutions. Cinema and retail are useful benchmarks for how you should change the customer experience. We are not in the trade show, events, or media business; our job is to connect buyers and sellers and provide information they can use to do business more effectively," he explains.

We suggested different ways to establish a yearlong digital presence for events in Chapter 5. We talked about creating digital platforms or marketplaces in house, licensing existing Software as a Service (SaaS) solutions or developing partnerships with commerce incumbents in the same vertical. In any of these scenarios, organizers need to incorporate digital and tech skills into their organizations and/or partner with the right tech companies. For many event organizers, it is unrealistic to think that they will be able to serve their communities OOO without strategic partnerships. These alliances will differ case by case, industry by industry, and geography by geography. Nevertheless, tech partners, as a rule, can help organizers in those areas in which most lack expertise.

Do You Trust Your Event Organizer as a Technology Provider?

Brands trust good event organizers to deliver value, attracting the right buyers and helping to generate leads and networking opportunities.

Trusting event organizers to be equally sophisticated software developers or tech companies is a different thing. Various leading organizers learned this in a hard way. That is because building turnkey OOO solutions internally without software company DNA is extremely difficult. Attracting the right tech talent, as event organizations, is also challenging since many top coders and engineers would prefer working for pure tech companies or startups. On paper, partnerships between event organizers and technology companies look good. In reality, they can be challenging. UBM Asia partnered with Alibaba in marketplaces, bringing two market leaders together, but the venture ultimately failed, as shown in our next case study.

CASE STUDY
ALIBABA AND UBM JOINT VENTURE

Summary

Alibaba and UBM attempted to combine their leadership positions in online marketplaces and exhibitions through an online-to-offline-to-online "O2O2O" model in 2015–2016.

Objective

Explore integrating the online and offline customer journeys to enhance the user experience and drive revenues for both partners.

UBM Asia: Fast track online B2B marketplace development with support from Alibaba to build a user-friendly platform alongside its tradeshows with increased traffic and user engagement

Alibaba: Utilize UBM's exhibitor and attendee contacts to improve supplier/ buyer quality and content quality across its horizontal B2B marketplace

The Joint Venture

UBM Asia and Alibaba joined forces in 2015 to combine their respective areas of expertise, databases and relationships. The joint venture gave selected UBM Asia trade fairs transaction and business portal functionalities. Other potential long-term goals included matchmaking, cross-promotional marketing, and audience development.

The "O2O2O" application was debuted in September 2016 at the Sign & LED China show. Although declared a strategic success, it failed to reach its full potential commercially. The pilot platform lacked sufficient traction with exhibitors and attendees. Put simply, there was not enough online traffic.

O2O2O Challenges

Lack of quality content

- 90 percent of UBM Asia's exhibitors were unprepared or unable to build a professional online presence with quality content. Some major exhibitors were hesitant to associate their brand with Alibaba, due to its reputation for low-quality products and fake suppliers and buyers

Low usability of the pilot platform

- The user interface was neither attractive nor user-friendly. Alibaba added numerous verification steps, making the platform difficult to use

Database mismatch

- UBM Asia had a relatively small exhibitor and attendee database compared to Alibaba's massive dataset. It failed to meet Alibaba's expectation for online traffic volumes

Marketing and customer success resource

- UBM Asia was not able to hire a dedicated sales team of perhaps 100 reps to roll out the new platform. Alibaba had thousands of reps, but they were not well suited to promoting the venture

Expectation mismatch

- UBM Asia expected Alibaba to help generate online traffic rapidly, while Alibaba was primarily interested in UBM Asia's B2B show contacts

Culture and Business Model Challenges

Verticalization

- UBM took a tailored approach to each vertical, focusing on the quality of qualified contacts. Alibaba operated with a standard approach across verticals

Scalability

- Alibaba expected scalability based on a standard platform across verticals. This approach works for B2C and C2C ecommerce. It was less useful for B2B ecommerce, which calls for a more vertical-specific approach

Team changes

- The tech giant had numerous joint ventures and projects running in parallel and it was comfortable with frequent changes to its project team. The O2O2O project did not receive the full attention of Alibaba leadership

Go to market approach

- UBM and Alibaba took differing sales and marketing approaches. Each had very different structures, channels, training, and personnel

The Outcome

UBM and Alibaba made the mutual decision to end the O2O2O joint Venture after the trial due to low online traffic, expectation mismatches, and management complications. The year 2016 was too early for the "O2O2O" model to deliver commercial benefits. Nonetheless, both parties still believe in its potential.

Alibaba and CCPIT Shanghai established a similar joint venture in 2020 for virtual events and e-directories, using the consumer show, Auto Shanghai, as a pilot. Alibaba's advertised role is to provide support with its AI, Cloud, and Big Data capabilities to enhance the exhibitor and visitor experience online through 3D modeling, mixed reality (MR), and augmented reality (AR) technology. UBM Asia continues to experiment with new ways of integrating digital tools and marketplace concepts, seeking to broaden its reach beyond events.

Lessons Learnt

Verticalization

A successful B2B online platform requires an in-depth understanding of the specific supply chain and buying behavior. Organizers may consider partnering with leading marketplaces in their target market to ensure they meet the specific needs of their users.

Broad-based, horizontal marketplaces typically lack the knowledge to offer content and services that meet the specific needs of buyers in a vertical market. The ex-President and CEO of UBM Asia says, "Verticalization is the only way. You need to have a perfect understanding of the vertical's value chain to deliver a successful B2B platform. Who are the buyers? How do they buy? Where and when do they buy? For an online platform, you need an even more in-depth understanding than show organizers [typically have]."

Content first: Quality content, of both suppliers and products, is the key to driving visitor/buyer engagement and ramping up platform traffic. "Quality content and up to date, complete product descriptions are key to attract buyers to visit, spend time and request proposals on the B2B platform," explains UBM Asia's ex-president and CEO.

Customer success

Exhibitors are aware of the importance of a professional online presence, but they need support from show organizers to deliver it. "More companies now will be interested in having a professional online presence. We observe the trends in other online channels. There will be more dedicated attention from exhibitors to deliver quality content," UBM Asia's former chief executive says.

Organizer mindset

The necessary content-led and customer success mindset is not natural to most organizers. It is a new skill for organizers to broker highly relevant content across multiple marketing channels (trade shows, online platforms, press, etc.) to attract highly qualified buyers.

Organizers interested in exploring OOO should identify their core assets, customer needs, and value proposition as a company and direct the right internal resources toward delivering on the OOO promise. Investing time and resources in long-term, complementary partnerships is critical to providing the OOO experience to customers.

Event investors, attendees, speakers, vendors, or venues, should demand OOO from event organizers to maximize their ROI and improve the overall event experience.

Conclusions

- Like many other industries, the events industry is being transformed. Technology will play a critical role and it is also the most important opportunity for event owners.
- Events should no longer be focused on two or three days. They should provide year-round services to their communities and embrace new business models.
- With a new mindset, event organizers must identify 365 value propositions for their customers related to the core purposes of the event.
- In parallel, they need to bring in skills or partners to both play and win.

Chapter 8

How to Navigate in the New World

"Innovation distinguishes between a leader and a follower"

Steve Jobs

We have lived through two decades that have been about print to digital. We have seen a host of changes with pure play entrants and legacy businesses struggling and then either reinventing themselves or fading away. Digital dimes replaced print dollars. The center of value creation moved from Fleet Street to Silicon Valley.

In events, we do not anticipate disruption on the same massive scale, but we do see change and some disruption.

In print to digital, customers drove the outcomes as much as technology. They voted with their eyeballs and their clicks. Event participants will vote with their feet as well as with their clicks.

So, let's start with customers.

Customers

Face to face has unique advantages, many of which cannot be replaced at least in the near term, by technology or alternatives. But this is not an acceptable reason to stand still.

In Chapter 4 we talked about attendees, generational change, time pressures, and alternatives. We also discussed marketing budget holders and the wide range of pressures they are under, including the ever-increasing choices they have to deploy their spend, measure results, and so on. We also saw that exhibitors are, overall, less than happy with traditional events. Some can be considered hostages to habit and the fear of missing out (FOMO).

Successful distance working is now causing companies to re-evaluate the need for all their expensive office space. Some are considering replacing face to face working in offices with distance connection and technology. Naturally, they are now running that same slide rule over events, as well as other marketing channels and investments.

The bottom line is that all events businesses now need to look at their customers differently and figure out how to meet their needs better. As strategic planning and customer closeness go hand in hand, we will start by looking at that.

Strategic plan

For a long time, it has been possible for highly successful events to operate relatively isolated from an event-marketing plan and without a strategy. Instead organizers employ a plan and a budget. This is because event professionals are excellent operators, highly capable of executing to plan and problem solving along the way. Add a strong sales force and the formula is a proven money-maker.

We came across a survey by T3 Expo, an event services business. Survey results show that half of US associations do not have a strategy for their events (Exhibit 8.1).

An event strategy anticipates market developments and customer needs. It positions the event to meet those needs and targets specific customer segments with tailored messages and offerings. With this mindset and process, the event evolves with its market and customers, instead of just following behind and reacting to opportunities.

Exhibit 8.1 Lack of sophisticated event planning—US associations

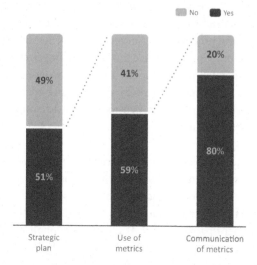

Source: T3 Expo, Heindrick & Struggles and George Mason University

Some single-sponsor events or corporate meetings (as opposed to third-party events) can be considered corporate strategy executions requiring no strategy of their own. Our view is different. We think that any event that has a brand should have a strategy. A strategy is essential to maintain the event's position and relevance.

Developing an event strategy requires understanding customers and the value that events can provide to them.

Understanding customers

All event organizers need a culture and a set of organizational processes that put customers first. Kai Hattendorf, UFI CEO, echoes this sentiment. "In my personal view, the key cultural element for a company in the events sector is customer centricity. As an industry, we build and operate marketplaces and meeting places—on site, and increasingly hybrid or online. We are successful when our customers can create good business on our platforms," he says.

Customer centricity means going beyond lip service. Many of us have seen highly detailed customer feedback surveys packed with pie charts that sit lost in the depths of filing systems. All too often in a mechanical process, these surveys don't ask the right questions. And asking questions just once a year is no longer enough. Even with the expanded range of tools from surveys and focus groups to analytics and a mass of ways to assemble and analyze data, the most important ingredient is a customer-centric culture built into the DNA of the business.

Some of the most successful organizers "live the industry." That means show teams don't think they are event organizers. Instead, they behave as part of the industry that they serve. It is like saying, "I'm part of the aerospace industry," as opposed to "I'm an event organizer in the aerospace industry." At a senior level, one leadership team we know of tries to make the cultural connection by leaving an empty chair, reserved for an attendee, in meetings. They turn periodically to that absent representative to get their feedback on proposals.

Sometimes, we see organizations appearing to lose focus of the most important goal of business events—to serve business needs. If they could only ask one question of customers it should be, "Why did you not sleep last night?" The response can help them shape a solution to the business problem through the services the event offers. Business information groups go to great lengths to study the workflows of their customers so they can understand their needs and develop what they call "use cases" for their services. More event organizers should look at a day in the life of a customer (DITLOC) or the overall customer journey to get real insight into their needs and frustrations.

Technology is a great enabler as we try to understand those sleepless nights and what the cure should be. But technology is a superb tool, not the end purpose.

With technology we can now observe customers more easily and learn from their behaviors. As Seth Stevens-Davidowitz explains in his book, *Everybody Lies – What the Internet Can Tell Us About Who We Really Are*, surveys are not reliable, but no one lies in the Google search bar. Our customers leave increasing volumes of digital exhaust from all the clicks and movements on their journeys, pre-event, at the event and after. This data can be turned into valuable analyses of their needs and preferences.

Data analysis can tell a story that is very useful for an organizer. But predictive analytics can go beyond the observable. For example, most organizers know that about half of those who pre-register for a trade show do not show up. Predictive analytics can highlight the high-value customers that are at risk so the organizer can take action to secure their attendance. Equally, we can now engage the other half that is not coming through different activations online and offline during the rest of the year. This expands the addressable market, allowing organizers to provide more value to customers.

There are now numerous self-serve analytics tools, such as Data Robot and Rapid Miner available to support this type of analysis. You do not need a data lake or a data scientist to use them. Data capture is not the problem. The challenge is with data organization and analytics, which are complex. Data without analytics is of little use.

Organizers should also use data-led approaches to assess their total addressable market (TAM). In the volatile fashion industry, former Advanstar CEO Joe Loggia grew MAGIC through industry cycles. It evolved from west coast menswear to cover most fashion segments nationally, as well as suppliers. MAGIC used launch, partnership, and acquisition to become the leading show. The business was sold four times, twice for over $1 billion. "The main reason for our success was data-driven decision making. We focused on the data and trends that drove our target customers' business results. We found who drives the influence and followed retail trends to identify the new opportunities. We took every player, classified and segmented them by category, tiered A, B, C, D. Then we dedicated a lot of effort to ensure that our internal processes and daily activities matched our data driven strategies," Loggia explains.

Loggia's approach is 20 years old. It is now common practice outside the events industry, but not in it.

We have noticed quite a bit of talk about design thinking. In our view, it is a fancy term for understanding customer needs and behaviors and then shaping a product or service to satisfy them. We find it frightening that there can be such a need for design thinking. Understanding customers should be central to the business. Unfortunately, disasters such as Comdex, CeBit, Interbike, and BaselWorld demonstrate the extent to which some events became divorced from customers and paid the price for it.

Now that we understand customers, we need to maintain relevance and engagement throughout the year.

Face to Face 2.0

By 2020 the divergence of the industry was fully under way. Two groups have emerged: those that are customer-centric and data-led, and others that could be described as "old school."

In most industries, a technology-enabled operating model is standard fare. It enables decision making based on data about customer needs and behavior. The more sophisticated organizers are investing heavily in systems to achieve this.

This is necessary in events as the task of delivering highly qualified attendees has become more complex. Some sponsors and exhibitors may have better customer data than a third-party conference or exhibition organizer. Also, events are now competing with highly efficient and sophisticated digital media investments. These pressures are pushing organizers to do a better job at showcasing ROI to their customers.

Easyfairs, which was established as a technology company focused on automation and customer-centricity, took its full leadership team on a fact-finding tour of Silicon Valley to stay up to date with technology trends. But they concluded that it was not actually technology that they had been looking at. "That was not a technology tour, it was a culture tour," says Eric Everard, CEO of Easyfairs.

The three enablers of a technology-enabled operating model are data, talent, and culture. Let's look at each of them.

Data is everywhere. The challenge is to capture it efficiently, know what you can achieve with it, analyze it thoughtfully, and use the results effectively. Yes, we know that is a big task. But as we have discussed, it's achievable in more ways than many imagine.

The challenge of finding, developing, and retaining top talent, the second enabler, is not new. The bad news is that it is only going to become tougher. It is common for senior managers to have ended up in events by accident. We think that bringing in a mix of new blood is healthy, but events struggle to attract the talent that works in tech startups or at Google. As Bob Gray, now operating Partner at Eagletree Private Equity explained, if P&G can make being the Brand Manager of Diapers appear attractive, surely the events industry can do better than that.

Exhibit 8.2 Technology enabled operating model

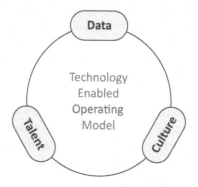

It is hard to generalize what the whole industry needs as human resource requirements vary so much across events organizations. There are big differences between brand owners, agencies, and third-party organizers, and between for-profits and not-for-profits. Nonetheless, we are confident that successful events businesses can expect to have fewer, smarter, better-paid people in the future. The talent pool will be very different, and it will have a new mix of skills.

The topic of talent segues easily into ways of working and culture. The organizer of the future will not talk about digital, just as today we don't talk about electricity. Certain skills will be endemic. Marketing will be at the heart of the organization, and social will be an everyday, effective tool. Analytics will be engrained in processes, and the list goes on.

The third enabler, culture evolves through a range of influences including history, leadership, type of product, and people. With so much success grounded in analog techniques, it is a challenge for many organizers to move to a customer-centric and data-led culture. The change will have to come from the top. "We have had 10 years of easy growth. Leadership now needs a whole different approach for transformation" says Simon Kimble, executive chairman, Clarion Events.

The New Mindset

Events businesses will need a new mindset to support the many new aspects of organizing. This means that they will operate with a different *lingua franca*. AMR International developed its Exhibitions 2.0 framework to help enable the transformation of the industry. It is described in Exhibit 8.3.

With the right mindset, a focus on the enablers of data, talent and culture, as well as an openness to changing the operating model, we see a path forward. However, looking at this in the context of Exhibitions 2.0, it remains a work in progress (Exhibit 8.4).

Exhibit 8.3 Exhibitions 2.0—a new way of operating

- **Multiple revenue sources** will replace booth or sponsorship sales
- The event will **reflect the industry ecosystem;** it won't just be an event
- The organization will be **attendee-centric;** it won't be sales driven, with booth sales at its heart
- Organizers will **innovate constantly,** seeking to be trend leaders; they won't copy-paste last year's format
- Organizers will be **data-driven and technologically enabled,** instead of making technology an afterthought
- B2B events will **facilitate interaction between participants,** and include matchmaking; random meetings will only be a small, additional and serendipitous part of the experience
- **Engagement with the community will be 365;** not just an event with a "see you next year" profile
- **Experience will drive advocacy,** with attendees serving as part of the marketing machine as opposed to formulaic marketing
- In the data-led decision-making culture, analytics and **predictive analytics** will become the norm. Judgement- based anecdotes and seat-of-the pants decisions will be a thing of the past
- **Pricing will be linked to value,** backed by specific proof points; the old approaches of cost-plus pricing or formulations based on gut feel will no longer be the norm

Source: AMR International

Exhibit 8.4 Industry progress towards Exhibitions 2.0

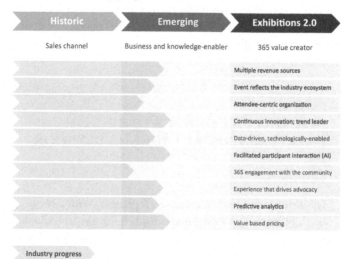

Maybe this is not for everyone?

We can hear some readers saying, "Is all this new-fangled stuff really needed?"

Many events businesses have functioned very successfully without sophisticated CRM, well organized databases, and marketing automation. They have used various combinations of market understanding, intuition, relationship-building skills, and guile to launch, grow, and maintain events. Cottage industry-like organizers are proven to make a lot of money for their founders. Indeed, looking around the world many hundreds have sold out to larger groups. So, why bother with all this expensive technology and new ways of working?

We see the answer as twofold. First, the old school approach may still work, but it will be increasingly difficult to maintain, particularly for events in mature markets with low growth and limited innovation. And second, there will always be room for the entrepreneurial launch.

Let's look at an example of an entrepreneurial launch. This is from Jay Weintraub, Marco's business partner and co-author of *The Face of Digital*. It is a different approach that goes against the grain of many corporate rules and processes.

CASE STUDY
INSURETECH CONNECT – THE
ENTREPRENEURIAL LAUNCH PLAYBOOK

Summary

Jay Weintraub is a serial events entrepreneur. With four successful launches and exits under his belt, he has a playbook, of sorts.

In his own words, here is how he used the playbook to launch InsureTech Connect (ITC). After its fourth edition in 2019, it was sold to Clarion Events.

Development	
Deep industry understanding:	Our secret sauce is to really understand the needs of the industry We spotted that tech-enabled transformation was starting, there was a need for change in the industry and with lots of startups were emerging
Connecting the people that matter:	We hyper-obsess over who needs to be in the room and how to bring them together. We look at the ecosystem of startups, venture money, incumbents, regulators, and so on
Big exclusion list:	We had a big exclusion list of who should not be there in year one. You have to tell the right story. You can't look like the others
Planned evolution:	We kept year one small to promote growth related to the content that is brought to the event. Customers grew with the event, at the first edition meeting their investors, then their customers at the next edition
Alternative approaches	
Not an events company:	We are not an events company. We are a movement; we are helping to effect change in the industry
Talent:	You can have events people, or you can have vertical experts. We had both, to get the best out of both Production is a commodity, so you can farm it out. The conference ops manager is the most at-risk person today as this mindset does not transfer to digital

Challenge formats:	We pre-built booths on the floor—no one was used to that
KPIs:	We measure conversations as the KPIs and assess how they will build over time
Invest in technology:	We invested in beacons that could track attendees and we integrated them with matchmaking
Pivot:	ITC was targeted as an expo in year one, but we got that wrong, so we gave away the space
Equity value thinking:	We had equity value thinking from the outset We had no business case, no budget. We just had a vision of the need of a group of people to get together

Conclusions

- Launching events is a very different skill than operating large events.
- There will always be room for entrepreneurs and industry insiders who are on the pulse of a sector and who can shape launches that are relevant to the moment.
- There are many ingredients to success, with customer closeness, innovation and risk-taking at the top of the list.
- Being digitally savvy, data-led, and analytical matter more and more.

The Event of the Future

Events are as diverse as the African continent. Event types will continue to evolve, morphing to fit customer needs in their markets. There will still be definitive events at which the whole industry meets, such as the Consumer Electronics Show (CES) or

The Farnborough Airshow, but overall, we see that events will be smaller when measured by physical attendance. Events will have a greater reach via digitally connected remote audiences, with a greater TAM. In the first instance, they will have less revenue due to reduced booths and sponsorships, but this extended reach provides an opportunity for greater monetization.

Let's look at the FreightWaves case study. This event is organized by event-industry outsiders. Its purpose is to stay close to customers. In the very early days of the Covid crisis, FreightWaves had no compass as it changed its model, always putting customers first. The financial outcome was a secondary concern, but it was far better than many others that had to abandon face to face.

CASE STUDY
FREIGHTWAVES: OUTSIDER SUCCESS

EVENTS AS A PROFIT AND ADDED-VALUE TOOL FOR CUSTOMER EVENTS

Summary

FreightWaves has been highly successful with both physical and virtual events. Much of this is due to its heritage outside of the events industry and its different approach.

Context

FreightWaves, founded in 2017, has rapidly grown into the leading information provider in the freight industry, dubbing itself, "The Bloomberg of freight." Its core business is SaaS delivery of freight intelligence. Media and events are also profit centers, but the organization's main goal is to build the brand and promote the business.

FreightWaves' event

Inspired by the success of Finnovate and Money20/20, Craig Fuller, FreightWaves' CEO saw a disruptive opportunity in the freight industry. The formula included quick-fire demos of the latest technology, keynote presentations from top-ranked speakers, and fireside chats, all centered around the intersection of technology and freight.

Playing to the Strengths of Virtual

When Covid required a switch to virtual, FreightWaves started with a clean sheet. It created a broadcast TV-inspired format with a combination of pre-recorded and live talks from thought leaders, product demos, and commercials. The duration of each segment was shorter than at a physical event. Dynamic chat rooms fostered engagement through informal discussions and networking opportunities among participants. The result was a vibrant and busy environment that kept participants engaged.

High-Quality Zero-Defect Virtual Platform

To create a virtual event that was more than just a decorated webinar, FreightWaves opted for high quality production equipment and personnel. To ensure success, the company sent broadcast-quality equipment to guest speakers and part-ners. The event was run at a production standard comparable to broadcast TV. "If you are going to ask someone to sit through a multiple hour or day event, you had better have high quality video and audio," the CEO of FreightWaves explains.

The Outcome

Success of commercials

Unexpectedly, the commercials between talks and demos were the highest-ranked content. The combination of relevant content and an ability to transition seamlessly between presentations were integral to their popularity. "In their (attendees') words, 'come for the game, stay for the commercials,'" FreightWaves' CEO comments.

Financials

The new format retained about 90 percent of booked revenues from the original event. It operated at about a quarter of the cost, delivering a margin of around 90 percent. Sponsors had exposure to a much broader audience and avoided all on-site costs, which delivered good returns to them.

Lessons Learned

FreightWaves, an outsider to event organizing, switched to a successful alternate format by:

- Reimagining the concept without the baggage of events industry thinking and focusing on what customers value
- Cutting no corners in production and execution, including investing to support customers so they could deliver television-standard broadcasting
- Treating events as part of a broader value proposition to engage their audience, add value and generate incremental profits

Implications for Events

Early TV was little more than a camera pointed at a radio announcer; TV today is hardly recognizable in comparison. In the same way, Covid-generation webinars and virtual will become unrecognizable with advances in production quality, content, and creativity.

Digital Tools

In Chapter 6, we looked at event tech in some detail; here we will look at its application.

We have established that some mass gatherings, live entertainment, big tradeshows, major conferences, and large corporate meetings are here to stay due to their unique qualities. This will remain so as they are professionally organized and organizers rethink what it takes to keep events alive and growing. If not, we will see many more Comdex-like failures.

All of these event types will be increasingly supported by technology to meet the needs of their customers. That is because event-goers now expect an always-on, touchscreen environments to be close at hand.

In an "old school" event, digital is predominantly confined to promotion, database development, and registration. Follow through

Exhibit 8.5 Digital tools improving events

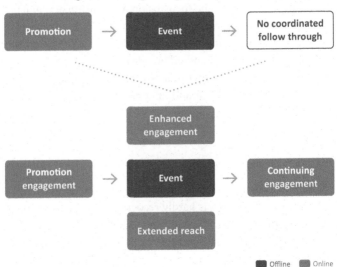

typically consists of reselling sponsorships and trade show booths onsite and delivering "see you next year" promises as participants file out of the door.

Successful events enhance engagement and extend reach with the extensive use of digital tools. The technology to make all this happen will be both invisible to participants through an improved back end, and visible to them via a seamless attendee journey that single sign on (SSO) kicks off (Exhibit 8.5).

As we can see from the chart, a full surround sound of digital tools will enable the event of the future. These are available and their capabilities and adoption is accelerating and extending.

Here are some of the ways that technology will play an increasingly integral and intimate role in events:

Before:	• Defining the shape of the event, its customers and their needs • Presenting the value proposition better • Marketing the event more effectively, with greater focus • Supporting the preparation of participants for a successful event
During:	• Improving connections and engagement, leading to improved outcomes (e.g., matchmaking) • Improved experience (e.g., wayfinding, AR) • Extending reach to those not able to be present physically (e.g., keynote streaming, remote engagement)
Post:	• Continuing the relationship with specific follow-through • Securing the value in relationships (e.g., lead follow-up and order placement)

With users engaging year-round through digital and other channels, in some cases, the event will become secondary. It will continue to fulfill a specific purpose in promotional and purchasing cycles, but it will function more as an annual celebration of the industry, an irreplaceable and valuable experience.

The event experience will continue to improve as business audiences increasingly require consumer-quality experience levels. Corporate events have been leading the way and this influence will spread further across other business events.

The experience is not just about pizzazz, food trucks, and designer gin, although these can help in the right context. The experience falls into two categories: the business experience and the human experience. Both matter, but we think that organizers will get the greatest bang for their buck from delivering the business experience. Think of the restaurant industry. Great surroundings can hardly ever make up for terrible food, but great food in terrible surroundings is more acceptable and can even be a winner in some circumstances.

Community Catalyst

Exhibit 8.6 Community Catalyst

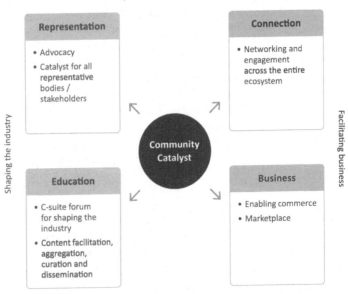

With the term exhibition now becoming too narrow, we now see an evolution from Exhibitions 2.0, an improvement framework that includes digital tools, toward a 3.0 which we call Community Catalyst. A Community Catalyst is far more than an event organizer, it sits at the heart of its community, facilitating the interactions that allow the community to thrive. We put the activities that it supports into four broad categories—community, business, education, and representation.

Many of these activities are in the remit of associations, although few take a holistic view and seek to act as community catalysts. For business publishers this concept is also less of a stretch than for most pure event organizers. Given their increased complementarity of skills, we think that we will see more convergence between associations, business publishers, and organizers. The tie-up between the National Restaurant Association and Winsight is a powerful example in this sweetspot of combined forces, each party improving the others (Exhibit 8.6).

Corporate meetings

The concepts we have outlined are valid in event types beyond exhibitions. Corporate meetings organizers are going through changes similar to those we have described. They too are moving from logistics to community management. In Exhibit 8.7, we have illustrated the progression that we see incorporate meetings.

Exhibit 8.7 What matters in the meeting of the future?

Illustrative

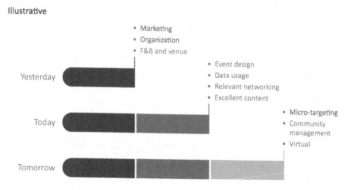

The Venue of the Future

We also need to look at venues and ask ourselves what the venue of the future will look like. Is it still OK to start with a box and have each new set of users fix it up as best they can?

After a period of substantial investment in venues around the world, including the mega venue in Shenzhen, People's Republic of China, venues now face the prospect of reduced event sizes for a considerable period. At the same time, everyone that uses them has ever-increasing expectations.

New generations of fans, delegates, and other attendees expect to have touchscreen, fully connected experiences in a convenient, attractive, and well-catered environment. The onsite experience, whether business or leisure needs to deliver through a mix of infrastructure, service, and technology.

Internet of Things (IoT) sensors, data analytics, cloud computing, Internet connectivity, and mobile apps will be standard. They will improve the attendee experience with better wayfinding, alerts, communications, and access to services and information. Combined with analytics, technology will allow the venue and organizers to gain insights throughout the attendee journey.

Organizers will prefer venues with "smart" digital infrastructure. Connectivity that supports large numbers of simultaneous users and bandwidth-hungry applications, state of the art digital signage and audiovisual (AV) equipment and a flexible local area network are prerequisites for the future. The Marina Bay Sands Hotel in Singapore has invested in an in-venue hybrid event studio. Italy's Fiera Milano has 80 high-resolution LED walls in its connected infrastructure.

Broad popular awareness of sustainability has put it on the agenda for venue operators. Energy-efficient, or even carbon-neutral, venues with intelligent energy management systems will be the norm in new construction. Waste reduction will also be tackled increasingly through reusable booths and catering supplies and the continued use of paperless processes.

We think that alternative venues will continue to gain traction. They provide a diverse atmosphere that can support the experiential aspect of events. Their quirkiness can become an asset for small to mid-size events in industries such as fashion and technology. For example, fashion shows are hosted in Berlin's old railway station and major tech events use the entire city as their playground.

AMR International created the Venues 2.0 concept with a vision of delivering the experience expected by modern, connected customers. The main aspects are described in Exhibit 8.8.

Exhibit 8.8 Venues 2.0

Venues 2.0	
Foundational elements	Advanced elements
Focus on customer success (organizers and event participants)	Unconventional MICE spaces
Seamless customer journey (organizers and event participants)	Smart building: process automation and intelligent infrastructure
Advanced digital infrastructure	Plug-and-play technology platform for organizers
Modularity of MICE spaces	Premium experience
Safety / security infrastructure (physical and cyber)	Iconic architectural features
Self-contained hospitality facilities	
Sustainability	

We expect to see more investment in tech-enabled venues as they seek to attract and retain business in an increasingly competitive market. The UK's largest venue, the National Exhibition

Centre (NEC) in Birmingham, was a major privatization success, which included reinvention, partnership, and investment. It was also a data-driven story as the NEC developed its own in-house-analytics team.

Expo City is a large-scale, high-tech venue planned for Las Vegas to host exhibitions and corporate events. It is designed to enable the future of B2B brand marketing by providing an immersive experiential platform for multiple industries. It also embraces the trend for brands to educate and inform consumers directly through permanent showrooms and installations.

Conclusions

- It is now essential for organizers to have a fundamental understanding of customers, not just survey feedback.
- The event should no longer be the purpose, but the annual celebration embedded in a 365-engagement strategy.
- It is a mistake for organizers to depend primarily on traditional booth sales and sponsorship.
- Event organizers should see themselves as community catalysts, not just organizers.
- Venues need to be intelligent and sustainable to be attractive to their customers.

Chapter 9

How to Structure for Success in the New World

> "Longevity in this business is about being able to reinvent yourself or invent the future."
>
> (Satya Nadella, CEO Microsoft)

Now we get to the part where the rubber hits the road. We must figure out how to deliver on everything that we have discussed.

The immediate problem of getting up and running again preoccupied minds during the Covid shutdown. While we don't underestimate the scale of that task, we focus here on what it will take to be successful in the new world, whatever that landscape turns out to be.

New Skills

We can't be sure what the new normal will look like, but we can be sure it will require a wide range of new skills. This applies across the board in consumer and entertainment, as well as B2B event categories, venues and service providers will need new skills also, but nowhere will new skills be needed more than in event organizations.

We already stated that it is a mistake for an event organizer to think that it is an event organizer. In the whitepaper, "How to Structure the Events Organizer of the Future," AMR International explains that an event director needs skills and capabilities akin to a brand manager at P&G or Unilever. AMR authors write:

"Apple identified its core skills as design and marketing and has been prepared to outsource the rest. Equally, event organisers should consider looking at the role of the event director through this lens. The core skill of an event director is setting a winning strategy and shaping the event in line with it, including defining the audience and determining how it will be delivered. The more time the event director can spend on this, the more successful the outcome. Other areas where the event director can add less value should be handed over in a client-provider relationship to specific centres of excellence within the rest of the organisation."

And now, the need is even greater. Event directors need to marshal an even broader set of skills. Operating as community catalysts and delivering 365 engagement are very different than event organizing.

EventMB's Julius Solaris agrees, saying that the role has shifted from event planner to event strategist. "Inevitably, the role of the event professional will transition from that of a list executioner to a more strategic, data-centric role charged with planning and executing experiences that achieve business objectives but also change attendees' lives," he explains.

This shift has only been realized in pockets. A leader in one of the largest global event organizations confided that only half of their people are equipped to think much beyond floor space. Other CEOs we have spoken to confirm that re-skilling and replacement of teams will be huge. As most organizers are operationally focused this will have massive ramifications for the industry.

We see the need to bring in new people with new strategies, data, analytics, and customer-connection skills. At the same time, many professionals in the industry will find their roles changing. Salespeople, for example will have to be more consultative, which means understanding the fundamental needs of each customer and determining how to solve their problems with a range of tools that include more than an exhibit booth.

Exhibit 9.1 Principles for a successful operating model

Principles for a successful operating model include:

- Customer intimacy and understanding
- Ability to realize economies of scale across the organization
- Investment in strategic capabilities that can be leveraged across brands
- Agility and resilience built into structure and cost
- Common technology and data platforms to enable digital and data-driven business models

New Operating Model

Organizers will need a new operating model that reflects an evolved vision, strategy, and culture.

We know that many organizers operate successfully in decentralized models, managing a series of shows as a set of largely independent small businesses. But with the growing complexity of the events industry and mandate for a more diverse value proposition, this template of joined-up cottage industries will no longer yield the best results.

A successful operating model supports strategic management and keeps brands close to the markets they serve (Exhibit 9.1).

In a successful operating model, we see the event director as a brand director, accountable for margin but also evaluated on customer success. This person has a mindset beyond event delivery and will be better remunerated for it. In many cases this calls for new talent. The organization benefits from managerial and other economies of scale, providing support for more specialist areas than for pure event delivery.

Organizational Structure

Most events innovation comes from external influences. Corporate events deliver a superior experience because they frequently switch agencies that are charged with keeping their events fresh. Startups and event outsiders such as ShopTalk or FreightWaves use a "beginner's mind" to adapt concepts from their own industries.

Overcoming the urge to cling to the known rather than explore the unknown requires careful thought about organizational structure. We see a need to reshape; considering separate units for new initiatives will be increasingly required to enable a sufficient level of innovation.

The Totaljobs case study, which is taken from the world of business publishing, tells a dramatic story of the need to create new structures and prepare to self-disrupt in a time of crisis. We are not suggesting that every events business go this route, but we see clear advantages of going a bit rogue when seeking to innovate.

CASE STUDY
TOTALJOBS: BOLD OR FOOLISH?

A STORY OF SELF-DISRUPTION

Summary

Print B2B publisher Reed Business Information (RBI) created online job board Totaljobs in 1999 when its highly lucrative recruitment advertising business was being challenged by competitors such as Monster.com. RBI purposely cannibalized a core line of business to save all its business.

Context

In 1999 RBI, part of Reed Elsevier (now RELX) was the leading B2B magazine publisher with over 40 vertical-specific titles in sectors such as aviation, IT, hospitality, and agriculture. Advertising was the predominant source of revenues with recruitment advertising enjoying particularly high margins. However, due to intense online competition, revenues started to decline by 2 percent from their peak of $400 million and margins declined by 6 percent.

Challenges

The emergence of online disruptors

The wide adoption of the internet heralded the demise of the B2B magazine sector. One of RBI's major revenue contributors, classified job advertising magazines, was challenged by online job boards. Platforms such as Monster.com were starting to fulfill the needs of recruiters at a substantially lower price point ($130 for an online job board post vs. up to $6.5k for a recruitment ad).

RBI's Strategy

Parallel offerings

RBI's powerhouse brands such as *Computer Weekly* and *Caterer & Hotelkeeper* sought to defend their leadership by creating their own online recruitment offerings. These were either sold as bundles with print or separately. However, this strategy did not halt the onward march of online competition.

Creation of Totaljobs

As pureplay online job boards gained share, RBI took the bold decision to create its own. Totaljobs had the mandate to compete with the disruptors.

This also meant competing with RBI's major brands.

Stand-alone business

Totaljobs was created as a standalone business. It was not treated as an online extension of RBI's classified recruitment advertising brands. It had a separate office and recruited a dedicated team with the specific skills required for an online media business. In short, it was separate and different to RBI's magazine publishing business.

Greenlight for self-competition

Totaljobs had clear permission to compete with RBI's classified recruitment advertising business; it could approach RBI's classified customers with its online proposition.

The result was that a recruiter in the catering sector could receive three independent sales pitches from parts of RBI— from *Hotel & Caterer* magazine, from *Hotel & Caterer* online, and from Totaljobs.

The Outcome

In 2012, Totaljobs Group was the No.1 job board in the UK

- The Totaljobs team had 350 people and a turnover of approx. $68 million and profits of $12 million
- It had 160,000 listed jobs and 7 million active jobseekers per month

RBI sold Totaljobs to StepStone, a wholly owned subsidiary of Axel Springer, in 2012 for $150 million representing approx. 12 times operating profit.

This disposal was part of a strategic divestment plan which saw RBI sell its B2B magazines to transform successfully from a B2B publisher to a data and paid-content service provider.

Lessons Learned

Totaljobs was a successful self-disruptor. The profit and value it created fell far short of that enjoyed by RBI's recruitment advertising business at the time, but RBI saw the writing on the wall. The investment in and eventual sale of Totaljobs helped compensate for the lost value of its powerhouse brands, which were declining as digital publishing and new revenue models were dawning.

Proactive self-disruption can be a valid strategy

If a superior value proposition will disrupt revenues, then a value preservation strategy can include self-disruption and cannibalization.

> "For a disruptable sector such as B2B publishing or events, if you don't do self-disruption, it will eventually happen to you and nothing will be left," says an ex-Publishing Director of RBI

Leadership in digital calls for a standalone business

When an analog group seeks to develop a digital business, it needs different skills, thinking, and culture. If it is not extricated from its parent, it can suffocate.

> "Those businesses which tried to roll out this paradigm shift from within their business failed," RBI's ex-Publishing Director explains.

Working with Event Tech

The new world requires cohesion not division. It is no longer a world with event tech on one side and event organizers on the other. After a couple of decades of experiments between software companies (the geeks) and organizers (the old school guys) both groups realize that success can be only achieved through sustainable partnerships between them.

A continuing challenge is that different EBITDA expectations often lead to misalignment. Event organizers have short-term thinking, worrying about their margin for next year's events, whereas software folks may be five years away from profit and are looking for revenue momentum.

After a long period of relatively slow adoption, we have an explosion of successful event tech companies. With inbound enquiries up 10-fold at myriad event tech providers and a set of genuine, urgent needs in abundance, many thousands of successful collaborations are flourishing.

But in our research, we have come across a cultural divide between the organizer community and event tech providers, the organizers and the geeks. Sometimes, it feels as if we should establish a relationship counseling service! Here are some of the comments we've heard (Exhibit 9.2).

There are echoes here of John Gray's *Men Are from Mars, Women Are from Venus.* Partners need to understand their differences to get what they want from the relationship.

Organizers need to figure out how best to collaborate on innovation. This could be working with any combination of startups, colleagues or partners, always looking for a better or more effective way to structure a test or a pilot. Innovation should not just follow the latest technology. It needs to be business driven, preferably focused on attendees.

We think that organizations need a vision and values that support the development of innovative products. With a culture of innovation and a structure that allows it, they must try new technologies and prepare to fail. This openness to experimentation needs to

Exhibit 9.2 "He said, she said" Event tech and customer divide

Event organizer	Tech provider
"We are trying to force vendors to improve their UI / UX. They are not responding. Maybe we will build our own and patent it? It will give us a specific advantage."	"The challenge with most organizers is that they take a waterfall approach to their event technology, which results in long release cycles, missed deadlines and a slow pace of innovation. The yearly cycle of rolling out new ideas is not feasible in the technology world—organizers need to learn to move faster. Clever organizers are iterating faster, looking at the data and insights leading up to their event and making adjustments in real-time as opposed to waiting until after the event is over."
"Vendors all tell you that their solutions are perfect for everything, but in the end you have to work with the functionality that they give you and make it work as well as it can in the context of your event."	"Tech vendors are offering a platform and service—this requires a substantial amount of support to drive customer success. The difficulty is that everyone needs training—the organizer, attendees and exhibitors."
"I have yet to come across anyone from Silicon Valley that is able to understand the subtleties of human interactions at events."	"Organizers must become data-driven, senior management should ask event directors to report on how many people log on, their behaviour, the most common path, number of exhibitor leads qualified or unqualified, most-watched session, and so on."
"Yes, we select platforms on price. That's because some have completely unrealistic expectations with imaginary business cases with revenue sharing that will never happen. Also, there are none outstanding in any category and many are so similar and only 'OK-ish' that it does come down to price."	"Stop picking technology partners based on a feature comparison but understand what the vision is for a technology partner and whether they view the world in the same way as you. Commit to long-term partnerships of building that shared vision together learning and iterating along the way."
	"Organizers have been selecting their vendors based on price and on features. In the end, they buy on price as they have such low expectations."

come from the top, driven by the CEO. Leaders need to recognize that failure is part of innovation. It should not be punished. But organizations need to support them through bonus protection, an R&D budget for event tech or other mechanisms.

The most innovative organizations, such as Google, do not demand a business case or ROI for every innovation. Granted, this is a very different approach to risk management. Nevertheless, events organizers need to think more like tech vendors and hire product teams to help them avoid becoming enamored with the latest "shiny new toy." Technology companies solve the problems their customers define. Organizers must do the same.

Event tech is no longer a luxury. It is a critical need that will help organizers improve the added value at and around their events. They can monetize technology investments with a range of new revenue sources and increase the TAM for all events.

Management Events, a Helsinki business, has a culture of innovation that it used not just to pivot its services, but also to change its pricing model and enter new markets.

CASE STUDY
MANAGEMENT EVENTS
CATALYZING CHANGE IN 1-2-1 MEETINGS

Summary

Management Events (ME) is a Helsinki-based event organizer that was founded in 1995. It innovated in conferences by adopting a "delegate-first" mindset and being among the first to offer 1-2-1 meetings. It has invested heavily in technology, developing an advanced matchmaking platform in house.

During the pandemic it innovated quickly to satisfy customers, create new business models, and attack new markets.

Context

Beta-testing virtual

When attendees were unable to travel pre-lockdown, ME found a way to give sponsors what they paid for. The teams facilitated Zoom calls from the exhibit floor to attendees. To everyone's surprise, it was an immediate success. It gave ME the self-assurance to accelerate its hybrid event development for the long term.

> The CEO of Management Events explains, "We were able to practice the core of hybrid events pre-lockdown, which gave our team the confidence that we can continue to deliver our services via digital channels."

ME's Adaptation Strategy

Non-physical is different

ME is moving its portfolio to a mix of physical, hybrid, and virtual events, now seeing non-physical as a different beast. Sessions are much shorter, the content carefully curated to meet the needs of delegates and sessions creatively moderated to maintain engagement and attract quality audiences.

> "Don't try to take the physical world elements and mimic them in virtual. Everything for virtual has to be rethought. Thirty minutes in physical is five in virtual," ME's chairman says.

In a second step, ME stopped selling physical events until firm dates became available. This drove sales of virtual substantially.

Harnessing talent from within

The company provided opportunities to select staff who were keen to develop digital events. At first, they worked independently. Then, once best practices were established, they were integrated back into the business.

Rethinking the rules of business

ME is using a period of disruption to rethink its business model and pivot away from "events as meetings" toward "selling access to a target group via a subscription model." Sponsors are now presented with a different proposition: continuous access to a sought-after group of professionals via a mix of formats (physical and digital) as opposed to one-time access at a physical event.

> "Hybrid changes the rules of the business. We are developing the concept of selling sponsorship opportunities as a subscription to the target groups. Are you buying 100 banking CIOs in Europe with this price tag? It will break the traditional ways in which we will think, deliver and sell." – ME's chairman, says.

Benefitting from reduced barriers to entry

The lower setup and delegate acquisition costs reduce the barriers to launch virtual events. ME recognizes the opportunity for pure-play competitors to launch digital-only attacks. It is using its strong, new-found capabilities to grab a piece of the virtual pie.

"Show Me the Money"

Jerry Maguire in the movie of the same name would have liked the EBITDA margins of major stock exchange listed organizers that were consistently at 30 percent in the pre-Covid decade. In the future, in-person events will remain profitable, although somewhat less so due to reduced scale and higher costs in areas such as content, 365 engagement, and hygiene.

The events industry will take a long time to recover to its former size and the peak of 2019. The 2020 Recession, budget pressure, and new ways for participants to interact are all constraints. It took about three years for leading players and the most robust parts of the events industry to recover their former size after the financial crisis of 2008. Unfortunately, we struggle to see recovery in that short a timeframe this time.

Nonetheless, money will continue to be made across the industry. The distribution of profit has never been even, and the disparities will both continue and change.

Event tech

Event tech will be the big winner. After being constrained by conservative customers and limited demand for a decade, players with viable solutions have boomed in the pivot to virtual. They now have every chance of continuing that growth in the hybrid era. Hopin, Bizzabo, and others have achieved high valuations. We will see more firms raise money and many that have been struggling for years will now achieve profitability.

We see event tech remaining as service providers to the industry, playing a more central and highly lucrative role eating into organizer margins, but not competing for their role of organizer.

Organizers

Organizers will feel pressure as their events will be, on average, smaller and their physical reach will be less international. They need to invest in technology to further improve marketing, maintain 365 connection, and extend their digital reach. These costs will impact margin. We can expect some weaker shows and organizers to suffer, others to seek saviors, or fail.

We will see a substantial shift in revenues, with booth sales, the historical cash cow for trade shows, bringing in a smaller share of revenue as shown in Exhibit 9.3.

Exhibit 9.3   Organizer revenue mix

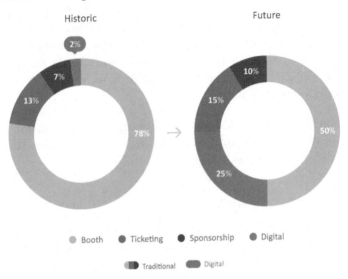

Source: Globex, AMR International

We will also see organizers expanding digital offerings and marketing services. These will range from full service digital agency-type offerings through to simpler packages such as EasyGo, the bundles of services including lead retrieval and digital promotion, provided to all customers by Easyfairs.

In the mid-to-long term, the outlook is positive for organizers. The pivot to virtual has shown that digital can enlarge audiences and improve participant interaction in some areas, such as 1-2-1 meetings with speakers and partners. Those that integrate with B2B marketplace platforms will extend their wallet share. These are all digital opportunities, so they come with attractive margin potential once fully monetized.

Exhibit 9.4 illustrates the cost comparison between physical and virtual from the point of view of an exhibitor, the sponsor comparison is similar.

Exhibit 9.4 Physical to virtual cost comparison

Illustrative – Based on constant organizer pricing

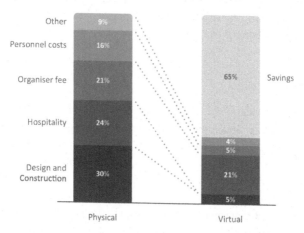

Source: AUMA, AMR analysis

Of course, this is just a guide. As the outcomes are not directly comparable, we cannot make a wholesale comparison of virtual to physical events. Nonetheless, this example shows reduced customer costs and illustrates the potential for organizers to maintain fees while reducing their own costs, leading to a margin expansion opportunity.

Venues

Venues will lose out. The Globex[1] data shows that while the events industry grew at about 5 percent per annum over the last decade, space requirements grew less, at about 2 percent per annum. We can now expect the need for space to decline as events contract and organizers continue the development of digital tools for customers. Venues make much of their money from ancillary revenue such as catering and parking, so reduced footfall reduces profitability.

---

[1]   https://amrinternational.com/what-is-globex/

The venues that will be best placed are those in major hubs, alternative venues, and tech-enabled facilities. There is an opportunity to rethink the venue business through tech engagement. An example would be working with in-house AV partners to develop sophisticated hybrid offerings.

Service providers

Service providers will lose out too. Their volumes are down and their organizer and venue customers, which are good at managing to margin, are passing along the pain. Physical service providers are downsizing and refinancing. Some that are dedicated to events may need to merge or close.

We see tech engagement as an opportunity for all industry stakeholders, so those service providers that engage with tech could find new revenue sources and opportunities to grow in the future. It would not be the first-time suppliers have changed lanes.

Broader Opportunities

The Covid crisis left customers who rely on events high and dry. They needed to go to events to do business—to find suppliers, learn about new solutions, and so on. With events canceled, they were not about to put a "Gone fishing" sign on the door. They needed alternatives.

The smartest organizers are thinking about this more broadly than just the lost space or sponsorship sales. They are looking at the total spend of their customers. Depending on the event type, that spend can be much higher than the fee that goes to the organizer. It can be as much as five or six times higher. They are trying to figure out three things.

- How to help customers reduce periphery spend. With less spent overall, customer ROI can improve
- How customers could deploy their overall event spend better to meet their needs. The organizer can offer other services designed to satisfy the needs of that spend

- Whether it is possible to access budgets outside events, that is, other parts of the marketing or sales budget, and if they have relevant offerings and permission to play. For example, targeting funds designated for obtaining leads and building brand that sit beyond events budgets

Among the opportunities, here, there are potentially some based on data. Events businesses are sitting on a mass of data; with the right focus and skills, events groups can leverage that data within their markets or across their organizations. For example, with data pooling and enrichment, events businesses can understand purchasing patterns of their target audiences, then with predictive analytics they can identify purchasing intent.

Registering for an event and then traveling to it is a clear sign of intent; this is the major advantage of the audience delivered to exhibitors and sponsors. We are now getting to the stage where organizers can predict intent independently of attendees being at the event. Alex Roth, director of strategy and business planning at Informa says, "So the role that events businesses can play in marketing services or supply chain facilitation is considerable. The value associated with those insights and services is very high."

Conclusions

- Revenues will come from services that are offered through the year. There will be a substantial decline in traditional booth and sales. Organizers should find new revenues in previously unexplored parts of customers' budgets.
- Organizers need whole new skillsets that deliver new services and generate revenue from non-traditional channels. These will take investment to build.
- The new world requires new operating models to deliver the services customers now require.
- Both organizers and event tech providers need to find better ways to work together, with greater mutual respect.

Chapter 10

A Conversation between the Authors

Along with a plenty of crystal-ball gazing and soul-searching, we have had a lot of fun writing this book.

We don't pretend to have the answers to everything, so we have spoken to a lot of smart people, researched far and wide and looked at fascinating case studies.

We have also had a lot of conversations ourselves. We debated the good, the bad, and the ugly. In this chapter, we are happy to share parts of our journey with summaries of some of our conversations and brainstorming sessions as we debated the critical topics for this book.

Why Are We Writing This Book?

Denzil: The older I get, the more interested I become in innovation. I really want to share thinking about what is possible. At AMR International, we've been doing that by launching the leadership event *Transform* a few years ago and then, of course, we created Exhibitions 2.0, a framework for improving events. So much of what we have been talking about has suddenly landed onto everyone's agendas.

And of course, you, Marco, are the person to co-write this book with—since you have been talking about event tech and innovation for such a long time now. And this is the moment.

Marco: After 25+ years in the industry and experiencing very few dramatic changes, I realized that the next ten years are probably going to generate many unusual changes (finally) and I wanted to be part of some of them.

Who Are We?

Marco: We have different skill sets. You (Denzil) are a strategic guy. You've seen thousands of case studies across your career, good and bad, successes, and failures. I am an entrepreneur and events operator. I still think like an operator every day even though I advise and invest in technology companies. Together, hopefully, we have provided a holistic view of what's to come.

Big Changes for Events; the Events Value Proposition

Marco: Thinking about the events business model, what are the main things that you see happening?

Denzil: It's a new mindset, with the event as the annual celebration, supported by a whole range of digital tools, year-round. I guess that a lot of it is encapsulated in Exhibitions 2.0 which we created to help leaders think how to do things differently. There is a lot to be done: strategy, digital tools, pricing, customer advocacy, and so on. But even that is not enough, and organizers need to evolve to a 3.0, something that we call Community Catalyst. We see this role as a joined-up approach to supporting an industry with lobbying, advocacy, education, contacts, and leads through tradeshows. To an extent, the community catalyst encompasses much of what associations are about.

But I don't see associations as being fully joined-up in that way. If you take an example from elsewhere, we would be saying to the French group Peugeot that it should be creating strategy as a mobility company instead of making cycles, scooters, and cars in separate entities and with separate strategies.

Looking at events through the lens of the for-profit organizer, we see their purpose as making money by putting on events and ultimately selling leads and connections. They too should be more than event organizers. They have to become entities that support the industry in whatever it needs. And of course, they can make money as a result.

As I have said, it is just a completely different mindset compared to being a show organizer that makes money by selling booths.

Marco: In my case, I spent time as a corporate event organizer during my early days at Apple, and after that, as a for-profit event organizer with my own company and Reed. I share your views on associations and their future role as catalysts and helping their members and their industries from a different angle, particularly if they embrace the right technology as a critical engagement and added value tool. After more than ten years of investing and advising event tech companies, I believe that tech will play a vital role in helping event organizers (for-profit, corporate, meeting planners, and associations) improve their event value proposition for the future. I'm pretty sure that we will see many successful event tech companies in different categories during the next decade, and I'm more excited than ever about the innovation that they will bring to our industry.

Big Changes for In-person Events

Marco: Now is a time that everybody is going to think, do I need to go to this event physically? Or can I attend some digital content from my home or office instead? This question was not relevant before, but it is relevant now, and it is going to force change in the business model. It is good and bad.

It is bad because, for those who have made easy money selling space, those days are now really over. It is good because smart people are rethinking the model and finding ways to generate added revenues from areas where it was almost impossible to do that before.

In the end, we're going to find a different business model, with a different revenue split and a different contribution margin that will combine face to face and virtual in hybrid experiences. And, we are not going to see a purely digital model where in-person events die. The pressure is coming from the customer now, and it is very loud and clear.

Denzil: I think for trade shows we're going to see space as a share of revenues going down from 80 percent today to 50 percent. That is deeply frightening for organizers who are running big shows. The winners are going to be event tech, and everybody else is going to be a loser. The question is by how much.

It is a scary time for everybody, it's all very well talking about the shift toward hybrid but putting this in place and executing on it is going to be a really big challenge. That's a challenge for the leadership who have been successful in the old world and also for the people throughout the organization.

This is where we get to the central thesis of the book— OOO—online to offline to online. That's the event of the future with the full surround sound of digital.

Marco: Yes, this is not just a set of tools for improved engagement and experience, we are talking about B2B platforms intimately linked to events. That includes marketplaces and the example of Informa Fashion and NuORDER shows the way.

Denzil: Ultimately this OOO thesis will strengthen events and in the medium or long term make them more profitable.

Marco: Absolutely! And I can't wait to see creative entrepreneurs and corporations launching new business models with OOO included as part of the value proposition. And I would also love seeing legacy events transforming into innovative models in the near future.

Virtual

Denzil: With Covid, we've seen the pivot to virtual. It's been a necessary stopgap, the downside being that it's really hard to make money from it, for now. We are pretty much all agreed that when face to face comes back, we are going to move to hybrid, that means face to face with a meaningful digital extension. So, would you agree that 2020 is the high point of virtual only events, with them only sticking around in some areas such as conferences?

Marco: I think that virtual is mandatory now as there is no other choice, but this will not always be the case. It's short term. It is good, as it is forcing people to think digitally first and create a model of engagement that is productive. Once face to face is possible again, virtual won't disappear, but it will shrink, and some organizers will keep the virtual assets alive so they can capture other value-adds from them.

Denzil: But to what extent will be standalone? I think virtual will mostly be connected to the core in-person event, so it's actually hybrid.

Marco: The way that I see it, there are three layers:

(1) On-demand layers that are super scalable and software-driven. This is virtual. I think it will still have a place and there is a lot of room for development, in the right areas, with smart monetization.

(2) Blended model where you have some virtual and some face to face. This is hybrid, and it will be the more powerful model as there are so many benefits for all stakeholders.

(3) Pure face to face but I'm pretty sure that the days for pure face to face without any virtual and hybrid elements are probably over. Customers should demand virtual and hybrid components as part of the event value proposition, helping them to improve their ROI and value received as part of their investments.

Event Technology: The Next Big Winner

Marco: Why are you (Denzil) so sure that event tech is going to be the next big winner?

Denzil: Up to now, event tech has been a really small part of the industry, and many of the event tech companies have not been very profitable. The events industry hasn't really embraced technology up to now. But now it has had to. Event customers have had forced choices, and now they are going to do things differently. We all agree that there will be a reduced footprint for in-person events as customers have found the benefits of some alternatives.

If you're an organizer, you have had to start engaging with event tech companies, sending them checks and using their services in a way you have not done before. Beforehand, a lot of organizers would have negotiated a set of free trials, not invested a lot and gone for the less expensive options. Now, they need to really embrace event tech properly, and this can only be a plus for event tech, of course, that's only as long as they choose the right partners.

Organizers are going to have to spend a lot on event tech. It is going to be a bigger cost to them than they are used to, but they will just have to deal with it. They are also not going to monetize event tech very well, at least in the short term. That's because they're still learning how. All of this means organizer margins are going to be under pressure.

They won't be alone. Venues will be hosting smaller events. There are going to be fewer delegates buying food and parking. Service providers will also find the going tough as their business models are mostly linked to the volume of face to face, and that volume is going to be down for quite a while.

So, I see everyone losing, except for event tech, who should—at last—be on a winning streak.

Marco: You know that I agree as event tech has been my main focus for the last ten years. It will be hard for me to believe it until I see it. Moving onto the competitive landscape of event tech, do we see event tech being in competition with event organizers in the future? Where is the line—is it just about partnerships?

Denzil: I don't see event tech competing with organizers. I think that organizers need to use tech and learn how to leverage the benefits. I think there could be some pure-play competition, from companies that aren't organizers, coming into the market as barriers have now been lowered. I believe that some organizers will attack others with pure online offerings, but I don't see event tech competing with their own customers. And the mega players in tech like Google have much bigger fish to fry.

Event Technology: Uniting Event Tech and Organizers

Denzil: Marco, Imagine that you're a marriage counselor, and you have event tech on one side and an event organizer on the other side, and they are not getting along which is clearly the case, what are you going to tell each of them to do to sort it out?

Marco: The most important thing is, focus on building the right partnership. A long term and sustainable partnership can be built successfully if both parties work together. Event tech continues to believe that event organizers are unsophisticated and old-school. On the other side, the event organizers keep thinking that event tech developers are geeks and don't understand the event industry.

If we could have a productive conversation about building a better event experience and earning a better return, we help each other. That is where the dialogue is more productive. I'm optimistic about more and better partnerships between organizers and event tech companies since we finally understand that both will need each other for sustainable growth.

Event Technology. Unicorns

Denzil: Why is it that in event tech there haven't been any unicorns? You just can't name a lot of big successful event tech companies? Is it because the management isn't good, the technology isn't there, or is there something fundamentally wrong with event tech?

Marco: You make a couple of good points. One is that people underestimate the complexity of events as an industry and the mindset of its customers. The customization that customers are asking for, in many cases, is killing the scalability of the product. The B2B decision-making cycle is also so slow and painful that many startups can't survive. And again, there is the fact that the events industry was in pretty good shape, which meant that event tech was a luxury and not a critical need. If you put these all together, there is a reason why you don't see too many unicorns around.

Until now, I think it was essentially a lack of interest and appetite from the customers, the buyers. Do I see more unicorns in the next ten years? Yes, absolutely.

Denzil: What if you now turn the tables now and think about it from the buyer's point of view? While there has been a lack of interest, there have not been any stand-out applications either. Much of that is to do with the complexity of so many different event types and the difficulty customizing implementation. Had someone created a silver bullet with some fantastic functionality, those buyers who weren't that interested would surely have latched on to the opportunity and made it work. So, is there something fundamentally difficult about making event tech actually work?

And who's fault is that?

Marco: Probably both—the tech guys and the organizers. If you talk with the organizers, they'll tell you that all the stuff that event tech is doing is cool and it's fun, but it's not moving the needle. And they're right.

Now on the other side, because of that lack of interest and lack of investment in tech over the last 20–30 years, they now need to build this "Frankenstein" in one year.

Denzil: As a non-expert, it feels to me that we've had about ten years in which there has been serious event tech and everyone in it has been working hard. Then surely by now something should have taken off and some people would be making a lot of money. That has not really happened, so why is it going to work now?

Marco: That is the problem; it is not going to work now. Event tech is about 10–20 years away from making a difference; and being fully integrated with the event experience. It has been around for a while and is very successful in generating efficiency and revenues in some parts of the industry. However, software and digital event tech is probably still 10+ years out from making a significant impact. What changed in the last six months is buyer behavior and priorities and a massive shift in the whole industry that will accelerate adoption. We will see decades of acceleration happening in months.

Competitive Landscape in Events

Marco: I believe that we are going to see new competitors coming into the space with a different model. I'm thinking about completely out-of-the-box players realizing that there is a clear opportunity for building P&L around events. They could come from any industry.

Denzil: Is there always this expectation that they will come from within a sector like Money20/20 came from payments, or do you see someone coming with a systematic process saying "I can launch across sectors, I have a process backed by technology, and I can do this now that barriers are down"? Or does the launch have to come from the industry where someone is an insider and actually understands the need?

Marco: I think that each industry will have players building these events. Each industry will have its own 2–3 of these players, like the FreightWaves case study we learned about. These players enjoy the luxury of not needing to earn a 30 percent margin on their events. They may say "I'm happy with 10 percent, or 5 percent," since they just want to be sure that the event generates value into the other revenue streams they have, whether it is subscription or SaaS.

I believe that this model is a real threat to the for-profit guys in some specific industries.

Denzil: I agree, though I think this is more relevant for conferences and confex, less so for scaled tradeshows.

Organization and Operating Model

Marco: The organization and operating model is going to change, but it is not going to change until organizers improve management skills and culture. What do we want to say about crucial messages around change and culture?

Denzil: I think the enablers of the operating model of the future are data, talent, and culture. Culture comes from the top, the CEO. A lot of these businesses have been successful for the past 5, 10, 20 years, and a lot of them have people who have been in place for that amount of time. Now we need a whole new skillset. Do we have people at the top of these businesses who can change fast enough? Or have their ways of doing things become so ingrained that they are unable to evolve and innovate? You'd maybe want to bring in new talent, maybe even someone from the tech sphere.

Marco: We still need translation; a pure tech person won't be a successful CEO in the events industry without coaching and help from more traditional event leadership and vice versa. Boards and senior management teams will need to include digital and events skills at a very high and sophisticated level in order to create modern cultures ready to innovate at fast speeds in any successful events venture in the future.

Denzil: Absolutely, you need someone in the middle.

We also heard of some organizers saying that they will need to change the skills and culture throughout their businesses. That means changing out half of their people if they are to be successful in the new world. That's sobering for many.

Long-term Outlook for Events

Marco: We have talked about a lot of change and a lot of pain for a lot of people in the events industry. I know that we both believe that face to face is not going to be replaced anytime soon, but what do you see as the long-term outlook for events?

Denzil: Once we are through the trauma, there are a surprising number of positives out there. We have had this emergency pivot to virtual, that has put event technology properly on the map and it can only improve events. I'm pretty confident that enough positives will stick, event tech will continue to improve with more investment and organizers will continue to figure out how to use it better.

Some virtuals have better levels of interaction than face to face with more speaker Q&A and so on. That's more valuable for everyone. Then we have seen this massive audience extension through virtual. At least some of that is going to be captured when face to face returns with all its digital extensions, in other words as hybrid. So that means sponsors and exhibitors will get access to more audience.

And don't forget that software is driving a lot of this, so that should be profitable for the software companies and for the event organizers too. Over time, I see the industry getting back to its former size and more and being a lot more engaged with its communities. That's an exciting long-term outlook.

Marco: I totally agree. I keep saying for a while now that digital technology is the best friend of in-person events, and now every single event organizer, exhibitor, and the attendees are realizing new and better ways to interact with their events communities using tech. That's fantastic news and will accelerate adoption and innovation like never before, creating new and exciting business models that will benefit all stakeholders.

Appendix 1

Case Study

PTTOW! A highly curated community centered around a flagship summit

Summary

PTTOW! is an invitation-only member network for C-suite leaders of major consumer brands. Its high resilience through the Covid crisis demonstrates the strength of a membership model supported by extensive beyond-the-event interaction.

Context

PTTOW! was created in 2009; it was built for CEOs, CMOs, and icons with the ambitious goal of establishing a community linking every major industry impacting culture. It has 350 active high-profile members including C-suite leaders of Fortune 200 companies. Icon members include His Holiness the XIVth Dalai Lama, Katie Couric, and Usher.

PTTOW! offers curated events of various sizes for community interactions, including VIP experiences at larger events such as CES, Cannes Lions, and SXSW, and exclusive research and insight reports. The crown jewel is an annual summit that incorporates think tanks, TED talk-like keynotes, dinners and parties, and bucket-list adventures such as training with the Navy SEALS or playing volleyball with three-time Olympic Gold Medalist Kerri Walsh Jennings.

One of PTTOW!'s metrics for success is the number of projects and partnerships that have come out of the community. These have included

Janelle Monae and Pepsi partnering for the Super Bowl Halftime Show to the creation of the Gun Safety Alliance, a network of business leaders committed to reducing US gun deaths by 50 percent by 2030.

The buzz of PTTOW! led to less senior colleagues of members to want to join. A similar membership community was launched in 2016, WORLDZ. Its goal was to connect WORLDZ members—the rising leaders of tomorrow—with PTTOW! members and to catalyze a positive cultural revolution. WORLDZ received traction quickly with membership expanding to 2,750.

PTTOW!'s Strategy

Quality over scale

PTTOW!'s membership strategy includes retaining C-suite executives from the top five companies from each of the 70 major industries it has identified as impacting culture, ensuring a wide variety of highly influential voices within the community.

Furthermore, PTTOW!'s invitation-only membership is capped, ensuring that scale does not dilute its core value. Management philosophy is that a community is defined by high-quality and fully engaged members. It believes that in a right-scaled, exclusive community, members can interact closely.

Roman Tsunder, Co-founder & CEO set out the quality strategy, "We saw that WORLDZ had become unwieldy after it grew quickly to 2,700 members. There wasn't quite the same sense of community there that we had with PTTOW!, so we decided to cut its member base back down to 700. That turned out to be the right thing to do."

Membership model

PTTOW! operates a membership model; it sees itself as a member organization centered on an annual event. The event is not the purpose—the purpose is building genuine relationships—although the event is a high point of the year.

Members pay a flat fee for annual community access, often signing up for multi-year memberships. This model has allowed PTTOW! to weather the Covid storm better than most other organizers with one-off, event-based pricing.

Staying close with the community

"How can we serve you?" is a common question asked by PTTOW's community managers.

During the Covid crisis community managers increased their connection frequency with members, offered each member insights and tailored services.

Covid-driven strategy enhancements

With the flagship event canceled in 2020, PTTOW! substantially expanded its community connection for the remainder of the membership year, through personal outreach and weekly virtual events. This created a model for an even more engaged calendar post-Covid.

In addition to webinars, PTTOW! launched a wide range of curated event formats with smaller groups of members. These were designed to drive more and deeper engagement. Additions included:

- Future forums; Q&A sessions with leading brands
- Think Tanks; intimate, pre-arranged sessions around a specific industry topic with spotlight "golden mic" moments for leaders of big brands
- Fortune 200 exclusive virtual round tables for insights sharing
- CEO & CMO forums for a small group of peers to meet on a regular basis

"These new formats allowed some members to change mindset from observing to actively participating", explained Roman Tsunder.

PTTOW! achieved high membership retention post Covid and is offering continuous engagement through events and related digital forums both to serve and to strengthen its community.

Lessons Learned

Curation of membership and content

Curation is an overused word, although the case of PTTOW! it applies. Membership is highly selective; it is invitation-only. Also, membership was purposefully reduced, leading to increased success.

Content is highly targeted and tailored to specific audiences—and often created with direct input from the members themselves. The expansion of content in the shift to 100 percent digital during the Covid crisis further increased targeting.

Membership vs. payment for the event

The membership model is powerful and robust; it allowed PTTOW! to weather the Covid crisis better than many others. Retention increased and financial performance was positive.

Although the community is centered on the event, the membership pricing model is fully accepted for the package which includes services beyond the event. This membership strategy interlinks with the community concept and more active participation of members.

Creation of a community

In many event organizations the focus is on sales; at PTTOW! the team culture is strongly oriented to serving the needs of members. PTTOW! has overcome the challenge faced by many organizers which is to form a genuinely engaged community. This has been achieved not just at the event but also beyond, creating a virtuous circle. PTTOW! is operating as a community catalyst.

Appendix 2

CEO Checklist—10 Things to Do

Although every events business is different, we see a set of common themes and have pulled together a simple checklist of priorities for CEOs.

(1) **Vision**
    Do you have a 3–5-year vision for the business that is markedly different to pre-Covid?
(2) **Strategies**
    Does each brand have a customer-first vision and strategy that defines its purpose in the community, which is known throughout the organization?
(3) **Value proposition and revenue model**
    Do you have a revenue model aligned with your value proposition as a community catalyst? Are you taking an OOO approach and defining new business models that will deliver a new revenue mix?
(4) **People**
    Does HR strategy define which talent is fit for purpose in the new world; is there a plan for training, replacement, and recruitment to create winning teams with the right skill sets?
(5) **Incentives**
    Are incentives correctly aligned, fostering a culture of innovation with reward for risk taking and not punishing failure?
(6) **Operating model**
    Have you redesigned your operating model to accommodate customer-first, digitally focused community engagement, as opposed to simply operating as an event organizer?

(7) **Data**

Do you have a clearly defined data strategy and roadmap, with data usable for analytics and a data-led decision-taking culture?

(8) **Marketing**

Is marketing at the heart of the organization and represented at the board; do you have a plan for digital skills to become endemic?

(9) **Metrics**

Have you updated the metrics and KPIs with which you are assessing the business, using forward-looking performance metrics that are digitally relevant and customer needs and satisfaction led?

(10) **Capital structure**

Do you have the right capital structure with the liquidity and financial stability for R&D, tech and innovation investments as part as your post Covid business plan? Has a budget for investment and R&D been agreed with your shareholders / stakeholders?

Appendix 3

Strategic Roadmap

Exhibit A3.1 shows a simple strategic roadmap which leadership teams can use to for their planning.

Exhibit A3.1 Strategic roadmap

Vision: Move from Organizer to Community Catalyst

Objective: [Statement about customers, value proposition and performance]

Priorities	Resources	Plan
• 1 ... • 2 ... • 3 ...	• People • Technology • Capital	• Year 1 – detailed • Year 2 – high level • Year 3 – high level

Do not boil the ocean

Revise annually

Appendix 4

Digital Preparedness Self-Assessment Checklist

Here is a set of questions designed to allow senior leadership to assess its position on the digital preparedness ladder. Baris Onay, formerly of ITE and Tarsus suggested this list to us, saying that it should get you thinking about your own approach to digital as well as how that might guide others around you.

About You and Your Engagement in Your Business

Ask yourself these—and be honest. These are about your behaviors and how they might be setting priorities without you noticing.

Organizational

- Do you have someone responsible for digital, who is not your head of IT and does not report to the IT function? Do this person have a team? Who do they report to?
- How often do you engage with your head of marketing? Does marketing sit at the board table? Who does marketing report to?
- Do you have a customer experience champion in your business?
- Is marketing a cost center?

Your engagement

- Do you browse your own websites?
- Are you on your marketing seed lists (i.e., do you receive all your outbound email marketing)?

- Are you following all your show social accounts (not having an account on X is not an excuse)?
- Do you register for your own events as an attendee? Do you like what you see? Who notices?
- Can you name your tech vendors (CRM, email marketing / marketing automation, registration and so on)?
- Do you keep a shortlist of digital experiences you like and want to see implemented?

Management process

- Does each of your shows have a separate, defined show strategy?
- Do you get weekly reports for lead generation / conversion, attendee acquisition and so on?

Intermediate/About Your Show Team and Their Digital Savviness

Ask your event directors these questions spontaneously. These will give you an insight into how important "digital" is on their agendas, and what gets prioritized.

Competitors

- Which was the best digital event that you have attended? Why, and what can we learn from them?

  - Webinar
  - Virtual
  - Hybrid

- Who has the best marketing? Why, and what can we learn from them?

  - Website
  - Email marketing
  - Social presence

Customers

- Which of our customers has the best marketing? Why, and what can we learn from them?

  - Website
  - Email marketing
  - Social presence

About us

- Highest converting marketing channels for

  - Attendees
  - Leads

- Metrics (% share and growth rates)

  - Mobile
  - Organic search

- Who is the biggest influencer in our served markets? Do we know them?

Advanced/Business-minded Tech Questions for Your Tech Team

Ask your head of Digital, Marketing or IT these questions. Expect direct, short and clear-cut answers. Do not accept long explanations. These people will enable your event directors (thus your business) in transitioning to hybrid of virtual.

- Do the attendee product interest categories on our registration forms map perfectly to the exhibitor product categories in our CRM?
- Do we have a data quality metric? What is it made up of, for example, recency, completeness, something else?

- What's the contact/account ratio in our CRM?
- Do we have a visitor and exhibitor data model?
- What's the average age of our contact data?
- What's the average age of our visitor data?

Index